Petrocelli

SAN REMO JUSTICE
AN EPISODE GUIDE AND *MUCH* MORE

SANDRA GRABMAN
FOREWORD BY BARRY NEWMAN

Petrocelli: An Episode Guide and Much More
© 2018 Sandra Grabman. All Rights Reserved.

No part of this book may be reproduced in any form or by any means, electronic, mechanical, digital, photocopying or recording, except for the inclusion in a review, without permission in writing from the publisher.

Published in the USA by:
BearManor Media
PO Box 71426
Albany, Georgia 31708
www.bearmanormedia.com

Hardcover: ISBN 978-1-62933-205-5
Paperback: ISBN 978-1-62933-206-2

Printed in the United States of America.
Book design by Brian Pearce | Red Jacket Press.
Cover Photo courtesy of Photofest.

TABLE OF CONTENTS

ACKNOWLEDGEMENTS 7
FOREWORD by Barry Newman 9
INTRODUCTION 11
PETROCELLI: A FAN SPEAKS by Max Allan Collins 15
HISTORY 19
PRE-SERIES MOVIES 33
EPISODE GUIDE: SEASON ONE 39
HALFTIME 79
EPISODE GUIDE: SEASON TWO 83
…AND THEN 115
CRITICS' CORNER 117
GOLDEN NUGGETS 119
TRIVIA 121
POST-SERIES LIVES 125
CONCLUSION 129
SOURCES 131
INDEX 133

ALSO BY SANDRA GRABMAN:

Spotlights & Shadows: The Albert Salmi Story

Plain Beautiful: The Life of Peggy Ann Garner

Pat Buttram, the Rocking-Chair Humorist

No Retakes! Actors & Actresses Remember the Era of Live Television

Lloyd Nolan: An Actor's Life With Meaning

ACKNOWLEDGEMENTS

My heartfelt gratitude goes to Barry Newman, who played the lead in both films and the TV series, and to Susan Howard, who played his wife and partner Maggie in *Night Games* and the *Petrocelli* television series. They graciously took all the time I needed to answer my questions and share their memories with me for this book.

Other people involved with the show also shared their experiences and/or photos with me. Among them are actor Michael Bell, actor Steve Eastin, writer/director Sidney Furie, Mrs. E. Jack Neuman (Marian Collier), Albert Salmi's daughters Jennifer Salmi LaRue and Lizanne Salmi Hansen, and director James Sheldon. Dalice Shepard and Richard Yokley also offered information and/or photos that were very helpful.

I very much appreciate the help of fellow author Chuck Harter who, while he was researching his own book about the television series *Mr. Novak*, did double duty on the West coast by gathering information about *Petrocelli*. It was a happy coincidence that writer/producer E. Jack Newman was very involved in both series.

Award-winning author, cartoonist, musician, and independent filmmaker (let's just say he's a creative gentleman!) Max Allan Collins is a huge *Petrocelli* fan and pointed out some elements of the show that I hadn't yet noticed. He was also kind enough to write an introduction to the book, entitled "Petrocelli — A Fan Speaks."

All photos, unless otherwise noted, are from my own collection.

FOREWORD by Barry Newman

It was a wonderful surprise to me when Sandy Grabman told me that her publisher had asked her to write a book about *Petrocelli* and that she was delighted to comply.

The years that Susan Howard, Albert Salmi, and I were filming that series were very memorable ones for me; and now, with the release of the DVD set, I'm being taken back to those fabulous years. What great guest stars we had, and what fine writing and directing we were blessed to have!

Sandy's book is magnificent! She took my memories, as well as Susan's and those of other people who were involved in the show, and is presenting them to you, the reader. I hope you'll enjoy this book as much as I have.

INTRODUCTION

This was the era of lawyer/detective shows: *Matlock, Columbo, McCloud, Barnaby Jones, The Rockford Files, Kojak*. Was another one really needed? You bet.

Attorney Anthony J. Petrocelli, played by Barry Newman, wasn't your usual Perry Mason. He was feisty. Bad guys tried to intimidate him. He refused to be intimidated. They tried to get rid of him. He very effectively fought back. The lesson? Don't mess with Italian-American lawyers who have a Harvard degree.

One of the two things I liked most about the *Petrocelli* series was that each case looked, at first, as if there were no doubt that his client was guilty. All the evidence was against him. What really happened was never as obvious as it seemed, though, and our lawyer-hero not only proved his client was innocent, but usually also made it easy to see who *really* carried out the crime. As each new clue presented itself, the viewers would start guessing how the crime was committed and by whom. Lee Winfrey pointed out in his December 22, 1974 article in *The Lexington Herald* that each episode contained three flashbacks: what the defendant said happened, what the prosecuting attorney said happened, and what Anthony J. Petrocelli said really happened. Tony Petrocelli might have been unorthodox, but he had integrity and would never give up. In the January 27, 1975 issue of *Variety*, Barry Newman told reporter Dave Kaufman that *Petrocelli* was a very difficult show to write because it had to fit those three flashbacks, a courtroom drama, and a personal, sometimes humorous, look at the Petrocellis at home into a forty-eight minute script.

The other thing that made *Petrocelli* unique was the warm, supportive relationship between Tony and his wife Maggie, played by Susan Howard. Maggie was a strong, but loving woman, a Texan through and through. She was Tony's partner in every sense of the word. Maggie served as his secretary/bookkeeper in the office, sometimes helped in the investigations, was there at the trials to offer her moral support, and celebrated with him when the cases were won. While they could be tough, each in their own way when circumstances called for it, Tony and Maggie had a huge capacity for love; and that love also extended to Mama Petrocelli, who called regularly from Boston, sometimes at the most inopportune times. Such beautiful family values aren't seen very much in today's troubled world. It's as if the show were saying, "This is what a good marriage looks like. *Do* try this at home."

Tony and Maggie.

At their service was Pete Ritter, played by Albert Salmi. An ex-police officer who had quit the force because of the chief's corruption, he joined the Petrocelli firm as an investigator who had resources all over town. Not only was he a star employee, but also a very good friend who continued to do his best for them, even when payment was slow in coming. The reason payment was sometimes slow was because Petrocelli would accept cases based on what was right, not on the client's ability to pay.

I'm convinced that, had the show not been pre-empted so often (seventeen times!), and thus had been reliably there for its viewers week after week, *Petrocelli* would have had a much longer life. Also, Susan Howard feels that, even though we'll probably never know for sure why it was cancelled after only two years, it might have been with us longer if had they given more time to the personal aspects of the story (family relationships, the building of their dream house, etc.). Nevertheless, viewers loved the show then and it has even more fans now in the United Kingdom where it's being shown in the new millennium. In fact, VEI/CBS released the full-series (pilot and all forty-four episodes) DVD set in late 2016. Consequently, even more fans are surely in its future.

PETROCELLI: A FAN SPEAKS by Max Allan Collins

I am honored and delighted to have the opportunity to be part of Sandy Grabman's fine tribute to the acclaimed, much-loved, too short-lived *Petrocelli* TV series.

I came to it by way of the film *The Lawyer*, which I saw when I was in college in 1970, going to the University of Iowa's Writers Workshop. I was commuting every day, so when I had a long stretch between classes, I would often take in a movie. I went to *The Lawyer* half a dozen times, fascinated by its true-crime basis (the Sam Sheppard case) and mesmerized by star Barry Newman's charismatic, quirky performance — you couldn't take your eyes off the guy.

I was also taken by the stylish direction by Sidney Furie of *Ipcress File* (1965) fame. He and Barry Newman together made the courtroom scenes fascinating and brought a hip contrast to the Southwestern setting, as well as crisp editing and unexpected camera angles. When I heard a *Petrocelli* TV series was coming to NBC, I was amazed and delighted — since when were TV executives that smart? Of course, the way they sometimes treated the series, maybe "smart" isn't the best description…

The TV version of *The Lawyer* continued the fascinating technique of attorney Anthony Petrocelli demonstrating an alternate solution to the D.A.'s version of the crime that indicated reasonable doubt, which meant his client must therefore be found not guilty. Visualizing the crime multiple ways was an extremely sophisticated technique for a network show of that era. And it was flat-out fascinating to watch a guest star be a cold-blooded killer in one version of the crime and an innocent victim in another.

Equally appealing was the loving relationship between Tony Petrocelli and his wife Maggie, so winningly played by Susan Howard. And Albert Salmi, whose work I had long admired, made a terrific rustic investigator to contrast with Petrocelli's big city roots. They were supported by some of the best guest stars of the day, with both Harold Gould and Ken Swofford from *The Lawyer* returning, although the latter in a different role than in the film (Gould's character's name was changed, but he played the same prosecutor in all other respects).

When the series originally aired, I never missed an episode, and when I revisited them recently, I found the series held up. The passage of time had not dulled the very modern feel of Barry Newman's performance, nor the cheeky boldness of Tony and Maggie's obviously sexually active marriage. The handful of episodes that took Tony out of the courtroom abandoned the *Rashomon* premise — possibly at the prompting of the network to inject more action into the show – but Barry Newman handled that kind of fare very well, veteran as he was of such hard-hitting films as *Vanishing Point, Fear Is the Key* and *The Salzburg Connection*. So those episodes made a nice change of pace.

For me, the best *Petrocelli* episodes showcased strong guest stars and revealed the lawyer as not only brilliant but compassionate — "Face of Evil" perhaps the prime example. "By Reason of Madness," "Mirror, Mirror on the Wall…," "A Very Lonely Lady," and "A Covenant with Evil" are just a few others. Choose your own favorites — the complete series now is available on DVD (although *The Lawyer* remains M.I.A. on disc).

I was thrilled to speak to Barry Newman not long ago, and found him as relaxed and warm as the role he played on my favorite early '70s crime/mystery show. He has been called "the Spencer Tracy" of TV movies, and I think that's an apt description. He was also an unlikely but terrific action hero on the big screen, where I first became his fan between classes at Iowa City in 1970.

Now it's time to enjoy Sandy Grabman's fun, informative valentine to the best lawyer series of the 1970s, and one of the best of all time. That's my verdict.

Barry with F. Lee Bailey.

HISTORY

There were rumors that real-life lawyer F. Lee Bailey would play himself in a movie about the Dr. Sam Sheppard case, but it was not to be. It was more important to have a professional actor in the role that wasn't meant to be Bailey at all. *The Lawyer's* writer-director Sidney Furie said he "was fascinated by the Sam Shepard murder case and decided to do a fictionized version." After having directed Marlon Brando and Frank Sinatra, Furie had said in the *inter/VIEW*'s article long ago that he'd "wanted to find anactor that I could push around…one of the breed that bide their time in N.Y. waiting to be discovered." When this was laughingly brought up much later during this book's research, Furie responded, "I said that tongue in cheek. I work with all actors the same and Brando and Sinatra no different. Both respected directors if you made sense. Barry was a pro and we had a great working relationship." The perfect actor for the title character of *The Lawyer*, Barry Newman was just as assertive as his character was. According to Kenneth Geist's *inter/VIEW* article about Furie, Barry had been so sure of himself that he told the director, "I'm your man, so don't waste your time looking any further." Newman lived up to his word.

The film, officially released in 1970, was a critical success and drew many more fans later, but was not overly successful at the box office. The premise was of a dedicated, intelligent, but often cocky and abrasive lawyer who left the rat-race of the big city to practice defense law in a smaller town. The movie dealt with a doctor who had been accused of murdering his wife. E. Jack Neuman originally had the lawyer's name as Vincent Zalingo, but it had evolved into Anthony Petrocelli by the time filming began. The movie's working title had gone from *Petrocelli: Lawyer* to simply *The Lawyer* by its release date.

Reviews were abundant: *Variety* was most impressed with its star, stating "Barry Newman, an actor who reacts, surmounts eccentricities devised to make him 'interesting.' He is interesting enough without them, and his debut has impact." *Film TV Daily*'s Herbstman singled out other cast members, as well: "Some of the characters in the film are cleverly individualized. As the state prosecutor Harold Gould turns in a strong flavorsome performance. Newman's wife and girl Friday, Diana Muldaur, is striking." John Mahoney of *The Hollywood Reporter* wrote, "Not only has [director] Furie cast the film expertly and drawn excellent performances from all of his cast, but he never compromises the performances gained to technical kitsch or directorial intrusion." He added, "Newman has style and charm manifest with a mime's discipline of expression, bringing the film some of its best laughs and emphasis in throw-away reactions and takes, carried by shrewd timing." Toni Gilbert, of *Entertainment World* wrote, "Paramount has a surprise package in *The Lawyer*, a first-class thriller which tops its own many assets by introducing Barry Newman to the screen." (Actually, Barry had been in two movies in the early 1960s, but this was the first one to showcase his talents.) According to *Life* magazine, "*The Lawyer* is a very sturdy entertainment." Charles Champlin of the *Los Angeles Times* pronounced it "a damned good little movie, fast, tough and interesting."

Why the theater made *The Lawyer* a double feature with *Romeo and Juliet* baffled Newman since the two movies would appeal to different kinds of people.

Everyone seemed to see what the filmmakers saw — that there was something very special about the main character. So, a television series was their next project.

Barry Newman, a Broadway actor whose heart has always been in New York, had been very happy to do the film; but when they started making noises about a Petrocelli television series, he dismissed that idea. By that time, he had starred in four films in which his name had appeared above the title — *The Lawyer, Vanishing Point, The Salzberg Connection,* and *Fear is the Key*. This was only television, he thought.

Planning for the television series continued. It would start with a made-for-TV movie entitled *Night Games*, which would also serve as the series pilot.

It was decided that *Petrocelli* would be shot in Tucson, Arizona. That would provide a realistic backdrop for the "eastern lawyer relocates to the west" premise, and the weather there was rarely a problem. They would need a building large enough to house several sets. Under consideration were the Old Tucson tourist site and the Brad Building, which, unlike Old Tucson, was within the city limits.

There were foothills and a clearing about twelve miles from downtown Tucson, near a rock from which so many Maureen O'Hara rescues had taken place that it had been named O'Hara Rock after her. There, in the clearing, they placed a trailer and built the foundation and partial walls of the house that Tony Petrocelli would be building, at twelve bricks per day, throughout the series.

About two weeks before shooting was to begin, Paramount-TV casting director Caro Jones went to Tucson to find as many Arizona citizens as possible who could be cast in the show. Hundreds of citizens came

The Indian Village Trading Post, as it was then.

to read for her at the Hilton Inn from 10:00 a.m. to 5:00 p.m., Monday through Saturday. She was delighted that more than 100 of them were already members of the Screen Actors Guild. Perhaps that was because the now-gone television series, *High Chaparral*, had originated there as well. Those with acting talent were sent to see the producers; those whose talents were in other areas could serve as extras. Teachers, Caro found, made very good character actors because they were accustomed to speaking before a crowd, so they wouldn't be distracted by the cameras and crew.

The Petrocelli office would be on the second floor above the Indian Village Trading Post at 72 East Congress Street. The first floor was, indeed, a wonderland of Indian items, which were popular with the tourists.

Petrocelli's first goal would be to get fifteen shows in the can. With luck and talent, the series would be renewed and they'd shoot more, they believed. Sure enough, in February came word that seven more episodes were needed, to complete their first season.

Writer/executive producer E. Jack Neuman was an amazing man. He was an advocate of extensive research to such an extent that he earned a law degree, but never practiced, so that he would be knowledgeable enough to write shows about lawyers in a realistic way. He did so first with the *Sam Benedict* television series in 1962-1963. Now he would do it again with *Petrocelli*. This was his baby, and he very much wanted Barry for the title role.

Newman and Neuman. PHOTO COURTESY OF MRS. E. JACK NEUMAN

To be sure Barry Newman was on board and to sweeten the pot a bit, they paid the actor $20,000 per episode and gave him control over the casting of Mrs. Petrocelli. He looked over the options and made a choice: Meg Foster. The casting director advised him that that particular actress was very good, but would be "repetitive of you, rather than complementary to you," meaning she could have passed as his sister; there was not enough contrast. Newman then saw Susan Howard and just *knew* she was the one. The casting director agreed; she was his choice as well.

Susan had already seen Albert Salmi in the 1958 film *The Brothers Karamazov*, but this was the first time she had seen Barry. As they worked together, there would definitely be chemistry between Barry and Susan that added a new dimension to the story. The fondness between the Tony and Maggie characters that we saw on the screen would be a reflection of Barry and Susan's real-life relationship. They both very much enjoyed working together and had the utmost respect for each other. To take it further in real life, though, would have been very unwise, both personally and professionally, so they wouldn't go there.

Being newlyweds, Susan and her real-life husband, Calvin Chrane, didn't relish the idea of the long separation that working on a TV series would require. So Calvin would relocate his advertising business to Tucson, doing most of his work by phone. Problem solved.

Everyone had a high regard for E. Jack Neuman.
PHOTO COURTESY OF MRS. E. JACK NEUMAN

Newman was also allowed to bring his own writer, Bob Hodge, with him. Hodge contributed much to the projects, but never sought credit for himself. His purpose was to take the script and put an edge to it the way Clifford Odets would have, giving Petrocelli a tough, 1930s kind of image. Barry's friend Jane Alexander had recommended Bob, and he proved himself to be very worthy of their trust.

Thomas L. Miller and Edward K. Milkis, executive producers, wanted Leonard Katzman to produce the show. Barry okayed that move. Katzman also wrote sixteen episodes and directed three.

Newman was able to convince the network that Petrocelli should handle more than just murder cases, but it took a while before they agreed to let him lose a case or two.

A childhood accident had left Barry Newman with a small scar beneath his left eye. What would normally have been hidden by makeup in other shows was, for this role, accentuated. Anthony J. Petrocelli was a feisty character who occasionally got into fights, so such a scar would be very fitting. Barry would grow to love his gutsy, sometimes abrasive character.

Susan Howard was perfect as Maggie.

The Rashomon effect — in which many witnesses see the crime in very different ways — was utilized throughout the two movies and the television series. Petrocelli's client was always the one who was obviously guilty because all the evidence pointed to him/her. It was Tony's ability to "think outside the box," and the exceptional skills of his investigator and sometimes Mrs. Petrocelli, that would work together to prove his client's innocence beyond a reasonable doubt.

Most episodes would involve three stories: the crime, the trial, and a personal look at Tony and Maggie. It was this personal aspect of it that Newman insisted on, and that made it a refreshing change from previous lawyer shows. The courtroom scenes would be filmed inside the

Pima County Courthouse, located at the corner of Church Avenue and Congress Street, on Saturdays, when it wasn't being used.

The Courthouse complex was quite impressive already when it was built in 1928 as the Pima County Courthouse.

It was designed in the Spanish Colonial style, with a pink stucco exterior and a tile dome atop, which was so fitting for that part of the country.

Barry's childhood scar was so true to Tony's feisty nature.

An addition was added to the south side in the 1950s, and the Presidio Park graced the front in the early 1970s. Now, in the 2010s, they use a much more modern building that houses the county Consolidated Justice Court, Treasurer, Assessor, Recorder and the Constables. Impressive still, but just not the same.

In *Night Games* and the resulting TV series, Mrs. Petrocelli's first name

The beautiful Pima County Courthouse of the 1970s.
ACESHOT1/SHUTTERSTOCK

was originally to be Joanne, then later Patsy. That would never do, felt Susan Howard. The character was a proud Texan with Irish roots. Nothing short of "Maggie" would work; so, Maggie it was. Hailing from Marshall, Texas, Susan was so happy that the writers incorporated much of her love for her home state into the scripts. Similarly, Barry's real-life Boston roots became Tony's, as well. At the request of Susan, they would insert some humor into her scenes.

Prior to meeting Albert Salmi, who would play ex-cop-turned-investigator Pete Ritter, Newman was warned that he would be difficult to work with and would "stab him in the back." The latter claim could well have been because of Salmi's brutal honesty. If he felt that a cast-mate was not a good actor, he would have no qualms about saying so. That was not a problem here, as both Barry and Susan were outstanding actors. They found Albert to be just as much a joy to work with as he found them. The three became good friends, and Albert loved to entertain them with jokes when the cameras weren't rolling. Because of his brawny physique, Albert had usually been cast in westerns as a bad guy or authority figure. In real life, though, he was the very opposite of this screen image. His daughter Lizanne said that, of all the roles he played in his very busy career, the personality of this

A very familiar part of the Courthouse for *Petrocelli* viewers.

one, the likable team-player Pete Ritter, was most like the actor himself. As Newman said in his Foreword of *Spotlights & Shadows: The Albert Salmi Story*, "Albert was unquestionably the sweetest, warmest, gentlest man I have ever known." Salmi's daughters say that he loved working on this series. The character he was playing was a refreshing change, and his cast mates were wonderful. Because his was a supporting role, rather than the

Albert Salmi and his character Pete Ritter were very much alike.

lead, Salmi usually worked only three or four days a week. He was a restless sort, though, so when he wasn't needed on the set, he would hop in his car and go exploring all over Tucson.

In a January 5, 1975 article, reporter Dick Kleiner told of his Tucson visit with this "Finn from Harlem." Albert took him to one of his favorite offbeat places, a restaurant called The Bum Steer, located at 1910 North Stone Avenue. Kleiner described it as a teen hangout, "its three floors filled with swirling kids were decorated with all kinds of junk suspended from the tall ceilings — even airplanes and sewing machines." Sadly, that restaurant is no more. It was sold at auction in 2014.

Newman too was very easy to work with. Director James Sheldon told *TV Guide* reporter Bill O'Hallaren in the May 17, 1975 edition, "A star sets the tone of a TV show, especially on location. Barry's tone is nice, warm, affectionate." Such kind cast-mates made laboring in the hot Arizona sun much more agreeable than it otherwise would have been. As Newman told *Tucson Daily Citizen* reporter Micheline Keating, "The most difficult part of this show is the elements, not the acting."

Even though his starring role was very demanding, Barry did have time off occasionally. One of his off-camera interests was tennis. He partici-

The Bum Steer had some glorious years in its past.

pated in a tennis tournament in Tucson during his *Petrocelli* years. Matt Welch worked at the El Dorado Tennis Club as host and racket stringer, and he recalls Newman coming in often. "He was a nice guy," Welch says.

Another of Barry's hobbies was playing jazz on the saxophone. In fact, he had been in the Army band when stationed at Ft. McPherson near Atlanta, Georgia. He emceed their shows as well.

Petrocelli would first be competing on Wednesday nights with *Get Christie Love* on ABC and *Manhunter* on CBS. The NBC show immediately preceding it would be *Lucas Tanner*. In March, *Petrocelli* would be moved to Thursday nights at 10:00 PM. This is when its ratings would go way up, becoming number one in its time slot and being watched by about forty-million people. In April, it was moved back to Wednesdays, filling in the 9:00 PM slot vacated by *Lucas Tanner;* and it would still beat out its *Manhunter and Get Christie Love* competition. The second season slot was on Monday nights at 10:00 PM.

Wardrobe would be mostly provided locally by Jacome's, which not only was located near the Courthouse complex, but was also generous enough to give costumer Thomas Welsh a key to their store for his after-hours convenience and a ten percent discount on their goods. This was quite a treat, since most stores that deal with the television industry have been known to jack their prices up.

As the series would progress, the scripts would get better and better. There was a lot of success ahead for this cast and crew. Among the many newspaper and magazine interviewers who spread the news about this show was Dan Lewis, who in *The Sunday Record/TV Week*'s September 29, 1974 issue introduced the series to his readers this way: "The lawyer cycle on television has just about run its course, leaving only 'Petrocelli,' the Harvard-educated, liberal, New York expatriate to uphold the honor of the profession on TV."

> Cast hired — CHECK
> Locations scouted — CHECK
> Publicity begun — CHECK
> Scripts written — CHECK
> Hilton hotel reserved for cast and crew — CHECK

It was off now to Tucson, Arizona for an adventure that would give us two glorious years of *Petrocelli*.

And it all began with a movie.

Barry Newman conferring with Director of Cinematography Ralph Woolsey.

PRE-SERIES MOVIES

The Lawyer
Movie: USA release date March 10, 1970

Director: Sidney J. Furie
Writers: Harold Buchman and Sidney J. Furie
Producer: Brad Dexter
Production Company: Furie Productions

MAIN CAST (CHARACTER):
Barry Newman (Anthony J. Petrocelli)
Harold Gould (Eric P. Scott)
Diana Muldaur (Ruth Petrocelli)
Ken Swofford (Charlie O'Keefe)
Robert Colbert (Jack Harrison)
Kathleen Crowley (Alice Fiske)
Mary Wilcox (Wilma Harrison)
Warren J. Kemmerling (Sgt. Moran)

STORYLINE: After a routine, everyday hearing, the judge told Tony Petrocelli that a murder of a doctor's wife had very recently occurred and the husband, Dr. Jack Harrison, was the suspected killer. Petrocelli went to visit Harrison in his hospital bed. The doctor was wearing a neck brace. He said that they had brought some friends home from a party for some drinks, but he was so exhausted that he fell asleep on the couch while they were still there. Sometime later, after the guests had left, he was woken from his sleep by frightened screams from his wife Wilma. He ran up to her room and discovered that she was being severely beaten by someone. The nap and drinks had blurred his vision somewhat, but the shadowy figure appeared to be wearing white clothing. Before he could come to Wilma's rescue, he was hit on the back or his head and passed out. Later, when he had come to, he was hit again, but remained conscious. He hadn't seen who hit him. When he finally came to, he went to his wife and discovered that she was dead.

Petrocelli read the police report, then went to the client's house with his investigator. They re-enacted the crime, with special attention being paid to the points in the report that seemed to indicate his client's guilt:

> His jacket, which had been covering him while sleeping on the sofa, was neatly folded. *(If he had woken to his wife's screams and run upstairs to her, he wouldn't have had time to fold it neatly.)*

> Harrison's watch and keys were stolen, but not the wallet in his back pocket. *(Burglary must not have been the motive.)*

> It appeared someone went through the drawers, but stacked them up neatly atop the desk. *(Staged to look like a robbery when it was just murder?)*

> Amidst the bed's blood stains seemed to be an imprint of a surgical instrument. *(Murderer was a doctor?)*

> Harrison's tee-shirt disappeared. *(The sergeant thought Harrison got rid of it because it had his wife's blood on it. He claimed it had been torn off him.)*

Was Harrison innocent? If so, how did it really happen, and how would Petrocelli be able to prove it?

COMMENTS: This movie was loosely based on the Dr. Sam Sheppard case, and *Boston After Dark* covered its special screening for Harvard Law students. Predictably, the young students objected to the less-than-idealistic presentation of the case. It was too graphic, too theatrical. Attorney F. Lee Bailey, who had defended Sheppard in his second trial, responded, "In a law trial, we call a spade a spade. If there's violence, we show it. If there's nudity, we show it." Barry Newman added that some compromises were necessary to make a good film. "A movie is essentially for entertainment, not a study in jurisprudence," he said.

Opposing attorneys Petrocelli and Scott were brilliant in their questioning. It was very much like a chess match. Scott would thwart Petrocelli's every argument, sometimes ethically, sometimes not.

Throughout the film, Tony Petrocelli constantly corrected people — even the judge — when they mispronounced his surname: It's *Petro-chelli*, not *Petro-selli*. That's one thing that would continue throughout the entire TV series. He was of Italian descent and proud of it.

Another aspect of this movie that continued through the series was the re-enactment of the various theories of how the crime was committed.

Diana Muldaur and Barry in *The Lawyer*.

That, and the fact that the one who obviously seems to have committed the murder, didn't, made this a very unique lawyer show.

What *wasn't* carried over into the series? Petrocelli's reckless driving and breaking of laws he didn't consider important, except for parking in reserved spots. He got away with that by putting signs on his windshield: "Dead battery. Be right back," "People's Exhibit A," and the like. On television, he treated others with more respect.

Viewer reviews on the Internet Movie Database *(imdb.com)* indicate some fans' feelings that this is leading man Barry Newman's best role ever.

Night Games
Television series pilot
"Saturday Night at the Movies," March 16, 1974

Repeated on August 10, 1974, as the lead-in to the Petrocelli *television series*

Director: Don Taylor
Writer: E. Jack Neuman
Producers: Edward K. Milkis and Thomas L. Miller
Production Company: Paramount-TV

MAIN CAST:
Barry Newman (Anthony J. Petrocelli)
Jon Cypher (Dale Hannigen)
Susan Howard (Maggie Petrocelli)
Ralph Meeker (Dutch Armbeck)
Albert Salmi (Pete Toley)
Henry Darrow (D.A. Jamie Martinez)
Stephanie Powers (Pauline Hannigen)

STORYLINE: There was a warrant out for Mrs. Hannigen's arrest for the murder of her husband. The police had already questioned her and now they were waiting for someone to bring the warrant.

Here's her story: They'd had a few friends over for dinner and drinks. After the guests left, they were then going to go to bed. Dale went around the house, turning off the lights, while Pauline went right to bed as she was very sleepy. In the twilight between wake and sleep, she sensed him puttering around, smoking while undressing. It was thunder storming that night. She had been asleep for about an hour when she suddenly awoke. She heard Dale talking to a man and woman whose voices she didn't recognize. She put on her robe and went out to see what was going on. She thought it odd that the window was open in the den and rain was coming in. She closed it and went back to the landing, noticing a tennis racket on the floor. She picked it up, then looked over the rail and saw Dale lying on the lower-level floor. She hurried down the steps, falling along the way, bruising her ribs. She went to him. He was dead.

The evidence was damning: $1,200 that the deceased had won in a golf match soon before his murder wasn't on his person and there was no evidence of a break-in. That meant the person who took it was already in the house.

The prosecuting attorney offered Tony a manslaughter charge, but was refused.

SUBPLOT: Maggie apprehensively told Tony that she was pregnant. She knew this wasn't a good time for an additional mouth to feed and was unsure how he would react. He lovingly let her know that it was all right. Later, he showed her the part of their future home that would be the nursery.

Pete and Maggie during a tense moment in the trial. PHOTO COURTESY OF MRS. E. JACK NEUMAN

Making a new life for themselves in San Remo, Arizona, the Petrocellis were starting all over again. Their homestead consisted of a mobile home, a brick house in the early stage of building, and much desert-land. Tony's goal was to lay twelve bricks each day and, eventually, they could move into their dream home.

An auto accident, caused by someone who didn't want Petrocelli to know and tell who really committed the murder, resulted in Maggie miscarrying the baby. Now that they had accepted the pregnancy and were looking forward to having a child around, their hearts were broken.

Stephanie Powers would later appear during the first season of the series.

EPISODE GUIDE

Series Creators: Sidney J. Furie, Harold Buchman, and E. Jack Neuman
Developed for Television by E. Jack Neuman
Executive Producers: Edward K. Milkis, Thomas L. Miller, and Ralph Riskin
Production Company: Paramount-TV
Wardrobe: Thomas Welsh, with assistants Shirley Cunningham and John Anderson
Shooting Schedule: Monday through Saturday
Formula: Three versions of crime, jury trial, and home life/humor
Network: NBC

Time Slots:
September 11, 1974
through March 12, 1975
Wednesday, 10:00 PM

March 27, 1975
Thursday, 10:00 PM

April 2, 1975
Wednesday, 9:00 PM

September 10, 1975 through ?
Wednesday, 10:00 PM

Weeks Pre-empted:
October 16, 1974
November 20, 1974
December 11, 1974
January 1, 1975
January 8, 1975
February 12, 1975
March 19, 1975
March 26, 1975
(This episode aired the next night.)
April 9, 1975
April 16, 1975
October 15, 1975
October 22, 1975
November 19, 1975
November 26, 1975
December 3, 1975
January 7, 1976
January 14, 1976

Series Regulars: Barry Newman (Anthony J. Petrocelli) Susan Howard (Maggie Petrocelli) Albert Salmi (Pete Ritter)

And now, at the beginning of each episode, we see Tony Petrocelli coming down the many stairs of the New York State Supreme Court Building (formerly the New York County Courthouse) on 60 Centre Street

Rosemary Forsyth, Barry, and Morgan Woodward.

and kissing Maggie "hello" on the crowded sidewalk, then the two of them in their camper crossing over the George Washington Bridge and heading west for San Remo to begin a whole new life away from the rat race.

The Golden Cage
Season 1: Episode 1
Aired Wednesday, September 11, 1974

Director: Joseph Pevney
Writers: Daniel B. Ullman and Leonard Bercovici
Producer: Leonard Katzman

GUEST STARS:
Joseph Campanella (Arthur Holbrook)
Morgan Woodward (Lt. John Cayle)
Rosemary Forsyth (Nancy Holbrook)
Fred Stromsoe (Alvin Day)
William Windom (Alex Mayberry)
Rose Marie (Thelma)

STORYLINE: From outside the mansion, we heard Mr. Holbrook telling his wife that she mustn't commit suicide because that would make him look bad. He then hit her again and again. She ran outside, and drove off into the night. She went to the Petrocelli home and asked Tony to get her a divorce. She said she was scared to death of her husband, and gave Tony $1 as a retainer. She then stayed with the Petrocellis overnight. The next day, they learned that there had been a murder at the Holbrook house of Alvin Day, Mr. Holbrook's assistant. She said she had heard gunshots as she was running out the front door.

Evidence against her: she had a firing range in the basement and was a crack shot, her fingerprints were on the murder weapon, and Alex Mayberry said he saw her shoot him.

SUBPLOT: This was about the case, too. Two menacing-looking strangers arrived at the trailer when Maggie was there alone, and blocked the door so she couldn't get out. They had some beer, then gave her money and left. Immediately afterward, Lt. Cayle charged her with hustling those two strangers and took her to jail. An obviously corrupt sort, Cayle had been the one to call the Holbrook homicide in to the police the morning after it happened.

COMMENTS: The last vestige of Petrocelli's bending of the law that made it to the TV series is parking near the door of the building and, in this episode, putting a bag over the parking meter.

The relevant cast and crew took to Tucson Mountain to film interiors of the mansion scenes in Brady's Castle, which was owned by William and Barbara Brady. This castle was built a bit lopsided to accommodate

Tony and Maggie at the desert site of their future home.

a 200-year old saguaro cactus, according to the *Abilene Reporter-News*. "Wasn't it fun seeing Bill and Barbara Brady's castle on the opening segment of 'Petrocelli'?" began an article in the *Tucson Daily Citizen*. It continued, "by the way, that was Bernie [Robbins]'s Lamborghini that guest star Rosemary Forsyth drove…"

A pre-premiere party was thrown for cast and crew shortly before this episode aired. It was attended also by Arizona Governor Jack Williams, his wife Vera, and executive producers Ed Milkis and Tom Miller. The governor presented the troupe with a welcoming plaque.

Music To Die By
Season 1: Episode 2
Aired Wednesday, September 18, 1974

Director: Paul Stanley
Writer: Oliver Crawford
Producer: Lou Morheim

GUEST STARS:
Rick Nelson ("Country Boy" White)
David Doyle (Cas Turner)
David Huddleston (Detective Ponce)
Jeremy Slate (Stacy)
Sandy Kenyon (Fred Morrow)
Don Starr (Judge)

STORYLINE: Country Boy White was singing for a benefit show. Once he had finished his set, he went toward his dressing room. He was encountered by Fred Morrow, who wanted some of his time. He was very persistent, so, in front of a bunch of young fans, Country Boy pushed him away, saying he's too tired. Morrow told him to meet him at the Desert Palm, #7, at 10:00 pm. A little after 10:00, there were shadows on a window shade of cottage #7: A man was pulling the dinner cart into the room, and another man came behind him and hit him hard on the head. The victim fell to the floor. When the waiter came later to pick up the cart, he found the body. The dead man was Fred Morrow.

There's plenty of evidence against Country Boy: multiple witnesses who saw him push Morrow and one who saw County Boy coming out of the Desert Palm, his fingerprints in the room where they found the body, and the fact that Jake Wiley had taken the rap for Country Boy in the past when he'd committed a hit-and-run with a bicyclist.

The testimony that cracked the case was that of the waiter.

SUBPLOT: This involved a multi-package shipment from Mama of various delicacies from her Italian homeland. After the trial, Tony was given the last package of the shipment. "Mama's provolone!" Tony said ecstatically. "Smells perfectly aged, too!" Not relishing the strong odor, both Pete and Maggie made their excuses and hastily left.

COMMENTS: This was the first of nine appearances by David Huddleston as Lt. John Clifford Ponce. This was also the first of fourteen appearances by Don Starr as the judge.

Barry with Rick Nelson.

By Reason of Madness
Season 1: Episode 3
Aired Wednesday, September 25, 1974

Director: James Sheldon
Writer: William Kelley
Producer: Leonard Katzman

GUEST STARS:
Lynda Day George (Vickie Richardson)
Loretta Swit (Ella Knox)
James McEachin (Dr. Herb Shoate)
Rudy Bond (Dr. Steinberg)
Rory Calhoun (Edgar Richardson)
Hector LeDesma (Jorge Cantrell)
John Vernon (Barney Majors)

STORYLINE: Vickie Richardson seemed not in her right mind when she told Tony that she killed her husband. She was very confused about the details, and didn't know why it had taken her five hours to call him, or why her husband was wearing different clothes than he did a few minutes before he was killed. The tux she said he had been wearing was nowhere in the house.

A man wearing a tux and a recording played at just the right moment solved the case.

SUBPLOT: The precarious condition of the Petrocelli finances was an ongoing problem because so many of Petrocelli's clients couldn't pay him. Pete told Tony that he had a heavy date that evening and needed money. Tony handed him a ten-dollar bill. "That's a good start," Pete said. "Now how about August?" "We'll talk about that in December," Tony responded. The waitress presented Tony with the tab. He had no money, so borrowed the ten dollars back from Pete.

COMMENTS: We learn an interesting bit about law when Tony was laying bricks on their future house and Maggie asked what the McNaughton Rule is. He said it's used when a person is declared sane or insane by a court. It's a dilemma, he said. It's just the opposite of "innocent until proven guilty." Using the McNaughton Rule, a defendant is considered guilty and sane until proven innocent because of insanity.

Having directed 110 projects in his busy career, it's rather amazing that James Sheldon remembered well his time on the *Petrocelli* set. He said they didn't spend a lot of time rehearsing, but rather would use the first run-through if it was good, or do a retake if it wasn't. He said that all three regulars on the show were very professional, and that he especially enjoyed working with Susan Howard. She was well prepared and, unlike many other actresses, did not hold up production, which was on a tight schedule. He loved his time spent there in Tucson, and said Production Manager Sam Manners "ruled with an iron fist, but if you stayed on schedule he was always very pleasant."

Filming the final scene of this episode.

Edge of Evil
Season 1: Episode 4
Aired Wednesday, October 2, 1974

Director: Irving J. Moore
Writers: Mel Goldberg and Dan Ullman
Producer: Leonard Katzman

GUEST STARS:
William Shatner (Adam North)
Harrison Ford (Tom Brannigan)
Lynn Carlin (Audrey North)
Morgan Paull (Daniel Carter)
Glenn Corbett (Robert Warren)
Robert E. Hardy (Judge Wannamaker)
Susan Oliver (Eleanor Warren)
Dana Elcar (Prosecutor Daley)

STORYLINE: Consumer Advocate Bob Warren had been shot in the back when his wife Eleanor came out from the bedroom to see what was going on. She had heard arguing between her husband and Adam North, and North now was holding the gun in his hands. He looked confused.

An illegally-thwarted building project and attempted bribery were involved.

SUBPLOT: The close friendship between the Petrocellis and Warrens complicated this case. Defending Mr. Warren's apparent killer was very difficult for Tony. When Maggie asked Tony not to take the case, he gently reminded her of long ago, when they were in college, she had said that she was glad that he was going to be a lawyer because the law is beautiful. He said he loved her for that because the law *is* beautiful. Tony said that if it's true that their friend was involved in blackmail, it would tear him up to pieces; but North was innocent until proven guilty.

COMMENTS: The *Petrocelli* series had many very big stars on it, some famous at the time and others who would become well known later. At the time this episode filmed, William Shatner was already a very popular and established star, known most of all for his Captain James T. Kirk character on *Star Trek*. Harrison Ford would get his big break three years later in *Star Wars*.

A Life For A Life
Season 1: Episode 5
Aired Wednesday, October 9, 1974

Director: Allen Reisner
Writers: William D. Gordon and James Doherty
Producer: Leonard Katzman

GUEST STARS:
Geoffrey Deuel (Edgar Dorsey)
Felice Orlandi (Lyle Holcomb)
John Anderson (Joshua Forbes)
Walter Brooke (Arthur Martin)
Henry Jones (Mr. Wheaton)
Eugene F. Coriell (Herbert Schleicher)
Sharon Farrell (Arlene Johnson)

STORYLINE: Edgar Dorsey was looking through the front door of the Hotel Congress, watched a man check in, and angrily went inside and asked proprietor Wheaton why he had a room available for that well-dressed man, but not one for him. Wheaton said he *still* didn't have one "for the likes of you." Dorsey said that he was dirty because he'd been riding all day, but he had money. "Out! Or I'll call the police. They'll give you a room, I promise." Disgusted, Dorsey went to the door, looked back at Wheaton, and told him that he'll be sorry because someday this place "will just burn on top of you!" We then saw the hands of someone setting fire to the contents of a large trash container, followed by Dorsey on his motorcycle coming out of the alley. A woman in the alley watched him go. Not only had the hotel burned, but an elderly gentleman named Herbert Schleicher was killed in the fire. Dorsey was charged with arson and murder.

It would be difficult for a rough-looking cyclist to look innocent, but was he?

SUBPLOT: Maggie and Tony had been dancing, celebrating their anniversary at a nice restaurant near the Congress when sirens blared the announcement that the Congress Hotel was afire! Later, in their home, she told him he owed her an anniversary waltz; so he started the hi-fi, but the electricity went out. Pete's electrician friend said it was shorting because of all the appliances, so their system needed to be replaced by a

220. The next day, Tony and Maggie were about to go to lunch together when the phone rang, summoning him to the police station. The next day, Tony and Maggie were having some anniversary wine in the dark. As they kissed, the power suddenly came back on in a blaze of light, as the electric mixer splattered batter on them and everything in its path.

COMMENTS: There is indeed a real-life Congress Hotel in downtown Tucson, at 311 East Congress Street, and that's where parts of this episode were filmed. It's a historic building, erected in 1918, and really *did* have a fire once that turned this three-story hotel into a two-story one. Perhaps that's what gave the *Petrocelli* writers the idea for this episode.

Richard Yokley, Tucson resident and *First Responders of Television* author, has details about the shooting of the fictional fire in this episode: "The fire station used for establishing with the Crown Firecoach apparatus (Pump 86a 1961 Crown F# 1253 Shop #60080) is responding from is that of Los Angeles City Fire Station 86 at 4305 Vineland Ave., North Hollywood. The actual Tucson FD does arrive on scene (note the Federal FH1 helmets) at the Hotel Congress and begin to stretch lines and raise ladders. The old City of Tucson city logo is clearly visible on the fire apparatus. In a scene where firefighters are spraying water

The lobby of the modern-day, though still very retro, Hotel Congress.
PHOTO COURTESY OF THE HOTEL CONGRESS/DALICE SHEPARD

into the hotel from the street is file footage (unknown production) of firefighters (wearing the yellow Topguard helmets of the LAFD) and appears to be filmed on a studio back lot. The studio lot hotel façade does not quite matchup to the Hotel Congress building. Later the Tucson firefighters bring out a body from the hotel on a gurney and place it into an ambulance.

"In your research, I am sure you have discovered the Hotel Congress and gangster John Dillinger connection."

And what was that connection? On January 22, 1934, Dillinger and his gang were hiding out on the third floor, using aliases, when a fire broke out on their floor. They were able to escape injury by climbing out onto ladders. Realizing then that they'd left their suitcases in the room, they asked the firemen to go back and get them, and they obliged. The suitcases revealed the true identities of the men, and Dillinger was arrested and transferred to the jail in Crown Point, Indiana. He escaped, but was re-caught and shot exactly six months later in Chicago — July 22, 1934.

Wednesday, October 16, 1974 — Pre-empted

Death In High Places
Season 1: Episode 6
Aired Wednesday, October 23, 1974

Director: Richard Donner
Writer: Leo Pipkin
Producer: Leonard Katzman

GUEST STARS:
Belinda Montgomery (Barbara Horton)
Stephen T. Blood (Al Smiley)
Harold Gould (Haskell Fox)
Richard Elman (Sam Horton)
Cameron Mitchell (Sheriff Bates)
Dick Alexander (Bobby Gains)
Barney Phillips (Frank Kelly)
Fred Ashley (Potter)

STORYLINE: A small private plane took off and, soon afterward, exploded. Aboard that flight had been Al Smiley and Sam Horton. Sam's daughter, Barbara, was the suspected murderer. She told Tony that she had driven her father to the airport. Pilot Smiley would fly him where he needed to go. The two men went off to file a flight plan, and she went into the office for an aspirin for her headache. Then she returned to the car and drove the men over to the plane. A mechanic was getting it ready for them, and Sam and Al boarded. They were about to take off when Barbara noticed that Al had left his briefcase in the car, so she ran over to the plane, went on board, gave it to him, then returned to the car. The mechanic closed the plane's door and they watched it take off. Why was she a suspect? Because "I'll inherit a lot of money," she said.

Evidence against her was the housekeeper's assertion that she had seen father and daughter arguing earlier about Barbara's wild shopping spree. Also, before taking her father's briefcase to him, she had gone into Kelly's office, where the hand grenade that caused the explosion was kept.

SUBPLOT: There were two of them this week. One was Pete's: Tony and Pete were standing before the judge, who listed the charges against Pete as public intoxication, disturbing a public event, and resisting arrest. His choices were ten days in jail or thirty days on the wagon. Tony chose the thirty days, much to his client's dismay. At the end of the episode, Pete was counting the days of sobriety he had left. Maggie teased, "You could always have ten days of bread and water." Pete responded that he was considering that.

The other subplot was Mr. Potter who, uninvited by the Petrocellis, was making a pre-test to see if the soil on their land would absorb sewage. He then poured water down a hole, and it absorbed instantly. He presented Tony with a bill for $105.25, including tax, saying if he didn't pay, he'd better stop building on that land. Much later, that same man came to Tony, asking him to represent him in a car-accident case in which he was being sued. Tony said that his legal fee was $105.25, including tax, payable in advance.

COMMENTS: The judge in the Pete Ritter public intoxication case was played by Arnold Jeffers of Arizona. This was his first screen appearance, and he proved himself to be a keeper. So good was he at playing a judge, he would return in fourteen more episodes in that role. Jeffers would then go on to appear in two made-for-television movies (*Go West, Young Girl* in 1978 and *Deadly Encounter* in 1982, both filmed in the Arizona/Mexico area). He would succumb to a stroke in 2001 in Tucson.

The judge for the murder case, who needed to take a brief recess to take some medication, was very pregnant. Tony leaned over to Maggie and whispered, "One of these days, Mrs. Petrocelli. One of these days." This was a reference to the baby they lost in the *Night Games* pilot-movie.

This was the first of six episodes on which Arizona resident Fred Ashley appeared. His was a very familiar face, even though he convincingly played six different characters on this show. Ashley's screen acting career consisted of two movies and two television series, all of which were filmed in Arizona.

Being Petrocelli's antagonist in *The Lawyer*, Harold Gould returns, with another name, in that same role.

The Double Negative
Season 1: Episode 7
Aired Wednesday, October 30, 1974

Director: Herb Wallerstein
Writer: Robert C. Dennis
Producer: Leonard Katzman

GUEST STARS:
Fritz Weaver (Col. William Fletcher)
Gene Tyburn (Tom Onslow)
Michael Burns (Billy Fletcher)
David Huddleston (Lt. Ponce)
Lisa Farringer (Renate Fletcher)

STORYLINE: Photographer Tom Onslow drove up to an office building and carried a package inside. Soon after, he was in his studio and on the phone with his girlfriend, Isabel Clark, who had been waiting for him at the bar. He heard a sound, so set the phone down to investigate. Isabel then heard a gunshot. She called the police. They arrived, saw Billy Fletcher there, discovered Onslow dead, and arrested Fletcher. Now with his lawyer, Billy told him what happened: Onslow had called them twice, never giving his name. He was blackmailing them for $30,000. Billy earned $550/month, and Onslow knew that, so he had to go directly to his overbearing father, the Colonel, for the money. The Colonel had it all planned out: they would go eleven miles down Old Post Road and leave the bundle of money on the high-tension pylon. The Colonel would then leave, and Billy with his motorcycle would be watching from a hiding place when the blackmailer came to pick up the money. Billy would then follow the guy to see where he went and who he was. He did that, but didn't stop there. Billy also, a short time later, went into the building to Onslow's studio upstairs. He went inside the studio and saw that the photographer was on the floor, dead. That's when the police came and arrested him.

The key witness that broke the case was a professor of Cinematography at San Remo University.

Left: Harold Gould, as opposing attorney Haskell Fox, was just as ethical as Tony. *Right:* Fritz Weaver as the overbearing Colonel/Dad.

SUBPLOT: The Petrocelli's camper had less-than-adequate tires on it. Tony had to borrow Pete's truck to go see his client, but it ran out of gas, so he hitched a ride in a milk truck. Later, at the Petrocelli office, Pete's friend, the tire man, had called saying if Petrocelli would do his little lawsuit, he'd give them four new steel-belted radial ply tires. Tony asked Maggie what the tire man's small case was about. "Selling defective tires," she responded. After the Fletcher trial was over, Maggie and Pete had Tony close his eyes and led him to his car with four brand new tires on it. It was beautiful! While Pete went to his own car, Tony and Maggie got into theirs, eager to take it for a spin. It wouldn't start. Tony yelled out the window, "Pete, who do you know that sells batteries?"

COMMENTS: Fritz Weaver was well known in show-biz circles as Broadway's Sherlock Holmes.

Mirror, Mirror, On The Wall...
Season 1: Episode 8
Aired Wednesday, November 6, 1974

Director: Irving J. Moore
Writer: Leonard Katzman
Producer: Leonard Katzman

GUEST STARS:
Stephanie Powers (Jean Carter)
Erica Hagen (Shirley Snyder)
Harold Gould (Haskell Fox)
Kurt Grayson (Allan Bell)
William Bramley (Milt Daniels)

STORYLINE: Young adults were having a fun time in the pool of their apartment complex until they heard loud arguing, then a gunshot from Allan Bell's apartment. Immediately after, they saw Jean Carter come out, then proceed onto the street without speaking to them. They went up to Al's apartment and saw him on the floor, shot to death. They called the police. Jean couldn't understand why she was arrested. She was nowhere near that apartment when he was murdered. The weapon was registered in her name, and they had six witnesses who saw her leave immediately before he was found dead. It wasn't looking good for her. Then a woman named Ellen arrived to complicate matters.

SUBPLOT: They received a phone call from Mama. She was coming to visit that very Friday. Maggie shopped, cooked, and cleaned, getting ready to welcome her mother-in-law. She wouldn't let Tony drive their camper near the bedclothes that were hanging to dry because it kicked up dust. She wanted everything to be absolutely perfect for Mama Petrocelli. At the end of a busy day, Tony and Maggie were in bed, declaring that they were ready now for Mama's arrival. The phone rang. Tony answered. It was Mama! She couldn't come. Tony told her how disappointed they were. After he hung up, he lay back down and said, "Wrong number." Having been fooled, Maggie pushed a pillow in his face.

COMMENTS: This was the second time Stephanie Powers, of later *Hart to Hart* fame, had played Tony's client. The first time was in the *Petrocelli* pilot, *Night Games.*

An Act of Love
Season 1: Episode 9
Aired Wednesday, November 13, 1974

Director: Paul Stanley
Writer: Leonard Katzman
Producer: Leonard Katzman

GUEST STARS:
John David Carson (Frank Donato)
Christina Hart (Niki James)
John Marley (Vito Donato)
Simon Scott (Senator Sam James)
Angela Clarke (Mrs. Donato)
Claudette Nevins (Annette James)

STORYLINE: The milkman, while making his routine deliveries, heard a window break, then saw a man run out of Niki James' house and drive away. He wrote down the license plate number and went inside to see if she was okay. She was dead. Frank Donato was arrested for murder. Here's what he said happened: He had a fight with his father, Vito, at the store. Vito hit him and told him to get out. Frank went from bar to bar, drinking. In one of them, the girl came in, recognized him from school, and came over. She didn't have a way home, so he drove her home. She invited him in and offered to make him a drink. First, though, she had to make a call. When she returned, she was wearing a different dress and a much colder mood. She clawed his cheek, then apologized and told him he could clean up in the other room. He went to that other room and began cleaning up when all the alcohol he had consumed that night caught up with him. He passed out on the bed. While still groggy, he thought he heard voices arguing, but wasn't sure. He went back to sleep. Something, he didn't know what, woke him up. He got out of bed and tripped over something on the floor and fell, shattering the lamp. His hand was bleeding. He looked down to see what he had tripped over. It was Viki's dead body. With his bloody hand, he checked for a pulse. There was none. He panicked and ran off. He knew he didn't kill her.

As the case progressed, politics came into it, shedding a whole new light on the murder.

SUBPLOT: There were two of them. The first was the strained relationship between father Vito Donato and son Frank. Vito had built up his Italian grocery business so Frank could carry it on for the next generation, but Frank wasn't interested in that. Tony urged Frank to let his old-fashioned father back into his life.

Barry and guest star John David Carson.

The other was the hotdogs that Maggie was grilling, when both Tony and Pete had been expecting steaks. They needed some paying clients first, Maggie told them. When the phone rang, they were hoping it was a butcher, needing an attorney.

Both subplots worked out nicely when the court case was over and Tony, Maggie, and Pete entered the Donatos' Italian grocery store. Tony had a wonderful time stocking up on his Italian favorites. They then went to the park to see Vito, and offered to share their vino with him. Frank joined them and greeted each person, his father last. "Papa, a game of Bocce?" Father and son then happily left to play the game together.

COMMENTS: Beautiful family values are a hallmark of this TV series.

Wednesday, November 20, 1974 — Pre-empted

A Very Lonely Lady
Season 1: Episode 10
Aired Wednesday, November 27, 1974

Director: Vincent McEveety
Writer: Robert Stull
Producer: Leonard Katzman

GUEST STARS:
Russell Wiggins (Albert Deigh)
Jack Ging (Wayne Jacoby)
Arlene Martel (Marnie Jane Underwood)
Lucille Benson (Angie Crawford)
John Milford (J. C. Underwood)
Robb Townshende (Percy Austin)
Louis Gossett, Jr. (District Attorney Kurt Olson)

STORYLINE: Police rushed to the crime scene to find the lifeless body of Marnie Jane Underwood in the desert and to gather evidence. The DA arrived. They lifted the cover and asked Albert Deigh if he recognized the dead woman. He wouldn't answer. The DA told the officers to take Albert away and book him for murder one. Deigh had just been passing through, working odd jobs along the way, when he became enmeshed in this murder. The evidence was strong against him: Her blood was on his pants and shirt that had been buried near the body, he'd been charged with felonious assault in Albuquerque and had also done six months prison time for auto theft in the past, and witnesses had seen them together the day of the murder. Add to that that Petrocelli's client wasn't always honest with him, and you've got a difficult case to win.

SUBPLOT: Maggie needed a winged leader flange pin for her sewing machine before she could mend Tony's favorite western shirt. Pete wasn't able to find one for them, but had a friend who could make one. Tony just couldn't, for the life of him, pronounce that thing. Fingle wingle pin? It was during the trial that Pete came in and gave the custom-made winged leader flange pin to Tony, who was overjoyed to finally have one. After the court session was over, Maggie asked where that sewing machine part was. Tony looked at Pete, who said he gave it to him. Just then, a police officer sat on it, yelled, jumped back up, picked up the small, but sharp object, and asked roughly what that was.

"The winged leader flange pin!" Tony exclaimed. Maggie and Pete looked at him with astonishment. He could say it!

"Is that yours?" the angry officer asked.

"No, no, that's not mine. I never saw that before in my life," Tony said quickly as he pushed Pete and Maggie along, hastily leaving the courtroom.

COMMENTS: Lucille Benson's was a very familiar face to viewers, and she appeared in four *Petrocelli* episodes. On our screens for over thirty years, she had a down-home manner about her — very much an Alabama lady. The scene in the beauty parlor between Tony Petrocelli and Lucille's character, chatty hairdresser Angie Crawford, combined advancing of the plot (by presenting more clues) with an element of humor. It was reminiscent of a Burns & Allen skit in which George was the straight man as Gracie talked on and on.

Counterploy
Season 1: Episode 11
Aired Wednesday, December 4, 1974

Director: James Sheldon
Writer: Edward J. Lasko
Producer: Leonard Katzman

GUEST STARS:
Ben Masters (John Delman)
Steve Eastin (Ed Miller)
Michele Conaway (Susan Delman)
Arnold Jeffers (Judge Maitland)
Stephen T. Blood (Ed Lester)
Gaye Huston (Wendy Burton)
Hayden Rorke (Atty. Arnold Cole)

STORYLINE: A gunshot rang out, then Susan Delman ran toward the road from the back of her house, screaming hysterically. Security guard Ed Miller, who had been patrolling the area, drove up, got out of his car, and asked her what happened. She said her husband killed a man and then took a shot at her. The officer told her to sit in his car while he checked things out. He went around to the back of the house, looked through the open door, and saw Ed Lester dead on the floor and John Delman, a police-officer friend of Pete's, kneeling down to him with his service revolver in his hand. "This is not what you think," Delman said. An inheritance, kidnapping, and shady lawyer were involved.

SUBPLOT: At home, Maggie's wedding ring had fallen off in a wheelbarrow full of wet cement, so she and Pete, elbow deep in the cement, were trying to find it. She didn't want Tony to know, but suddenly, there he was! When Tony asked what they were doing, both Maggie and Pete stood with their hands behind their backs, trying to look nonchalant. After some hemming and hawing, they claimed the cement was too thick so they were thinning it out. Something caught Tony's eye. He reached down to the cement and plucked out Maggie's wedding ring. He told her to keep it because they might have to hock it someday.

COMMENTS: *Petrocelli* casting directors liked to include Tucson locals in their shows whenever they could. Two in particular — Don Starr and

Arnold Jeffers — had an air of authority and dignity about them, so they were cast as judges. Steve Eastin, who had been teaching at the University of Arizona, was cast in this episode as the security guard. He was in seven episodes; and has been a very, very busy actor ever since.

The real-life Tucson restaurant, The Bum Steer, was featured in this episode.

Wednesday, December 11, 1974 — Pre-empted

A Covenant With Evil
Season 1: Episode 12
Aired Wednesday, December 18, 1974

Director: James Sheldon
Writers: Bob Green and Bill Harley
Producer: Leonard Katzman

GUEST STARS:
Charles Martin Smith (Frankie Toyer)
Paul Carr (Paul Cooper)
Robyn Millan (Beth Williams)
Julie Cobb (Millie Conway)
Dean Harens (Dr. Oscar Vinton)
David Huddleston (Lt. Ponce)
Arthur Malet (Clyde Ledbetter)
Arnold Jeffers (Judge)

STORYLINE: Beth Williams was coming out of the shower when she heard a noise. Someone had broken in. She crossly asked what he was doing there.

From the apartment-manager's office, Clyde Ledbetter heard her screams, called the police, then went to see what happened. He discovered her dead body on the bed and his mentally-handicapped helper, Frankie Toyer, cradling her. "Frankie! You killed her!" Clyde said. Frankie later told Petrocelli that, having heard the screams and checking on her, he shook her to get her to wake up. When she didn't, he picked her up and put her on the bed. He was afraid shaking her had been what killed her. He was so scared.

A boyfriend, a doctor, and a business deal figure in this mystery.

SUBPLOT: Tony and Maggie were returning home from a party in the early hours of the morning. While she went inside the trailer, Tony went to check on the progress of his homemade wine. Taking a taste, he declared it perfect. The next day, Maggie, Pete and Tony were at the Petrocelli homestead; and Tony was pouring his newly-made vino into glasses for them. One swig, and Pete spit it out. Maggie and Tony grimaced. It tasted terrible! How did that happen?

COMMENTS: When a woman had called about a parking question, Maggie had said jokingly that Tony's the wrong lawyer to ask about parking violations. That was an inside joke between the show and its viewers. In the opening credits of each show, we'd see Tony driving up to the nearest parking space to the door and covering the parking meter with a bag, propping the hood of his car up so the car would appear to be disabled, or putting a sign, such as "People's Exhibit A," on the windshield to keep from being ticketed.

Wednesday, January 1, 1975 — Pre-empted

Wednesday, January 8, 1975 — Pre-empted

The Sleep of Reason
Season 1: Episode 13
Aired Wednesday, January 15, 1975

Director: Irving J. Moore
Writer: William Kelley
Producer: Leonard Katzman

GUEST STARS:
Christopher Connolly (Willie Flanders)
Logan Ramsey (Prof. Beale)
Pamela Franklin (Joan Barth)
Francine York (Annabelle Tracy)
Albert Stratton (Prof. Logan)

STORYLINE: Willie Flanders walked resolutely into the university's auditorium, where Prof. Beale was giving a lecture on hypnosis. The professor held his pointer stick up and asked, "What do you want now?" Willie shot him dead. While students screamed and ran, Willie looked confused. He was a highly-principled teaching assistant; this was so unlike him. How on earth could Willie ever be found innocent in such a case? Annabelle Tracy shows us how.

SUBPLOT: *Warning: Spoiler Alert!* At the risk of giving away the mystery's solution, the subplot began when Tony, Maggie, and Pete went to see the show of hypnotist Annabelle Tracy. The Petrocellis volunteered their pal as a subject for Annabelle's demonstration. She hypnotized Pete into believing that, whenever the word "marbles" was spoken, beer would taste like turpentine.

Barry with guest star Christopher Connolly.

After the trial was over and the threesome was back at the Petrocelli homestead, Pete asked if they had any root beer. He said that regular beer just didn't taste as good anymore. He then couldn't understand why Maggie and Tony were laughing uproariously.

COMMENTS: Christopher Connelly would be back the next year in the very tense episode "Survival." His career was going so well until lung cancer cut his life short in 1988. He was only 47.

A Fallen Idol
Season 1: Episode 14
Aired Wednesday, January 22, 1975

Director: Herb Wallerstein
Writer: Leonard Katzman
Producer: Leonard Katzman

GUEST STARS:
Don Stroud (Frankie Copa)
Louis Gossett, Jr. (District Attorney Kurt Olson)
Susan Strasberg (T. J. Farlow)
Richard Ward (Charlie Bobo)
George Petrie (Morrie Ryder)
Ben Hammer (Arthur Handler)

STORYLINE: Tony went to a gym to say "hello" to visiting boxer Frankie Copa, who was an old schoolmate back in Boston. He had a few friendly words with him, then was hustled away from Copa by manager Morrie Ryder so the boxer could continue his workout uninterrupted. Ryder handed Tony off to Copa's girlfriend, T.J. Tony gave T. J. his business card and invited her and Frankie to join him and Maggie for dinner at a great Italian restaurant. He gave her the name of the restaurant and time they'd be there and hoped the couple would join them. That evening, they learned that Frankie had been arrested for assaulting manager Morrie. Here's what Frankie said happened: Morrie and Handler were arguing with each other as Frankie went to shower after his workout. When Frankie came back out, dried himself off and began getting dressed, he heard a low moan. He went to see where it was coming from and found Morrie lying on the floor, badly beaten. He knelt down to him and tried to slap him back into consciousness, but Handler showed up and accused him of attacking Morrie. Other men gathered around and held Frankie down until the police arrived. Morrie Ryder died that same evening, so it was now a murder case.

In the Petrocelli trailer, Tony, Maggie, Pete, and T. J. discussed the case. T. J. said that a company, Allied Sports International, owned boxers and managers, and the company got the money. They kept sixty percent of the profits, with Frankie and Morris splitting the remainder. They worked Frankie hard and constantly, with no rest. The Allied Sports lawyer tried to get Tony off the case, but feisty Tony wouldn't desert his friend.

SUBPLOT: The unshakable friendship between Frankie and Tony endured. Back in the gym after her boyfriend was released, T. J. said to Maggie that Frankie had only one more fight to go, then maybe it would be over. She so hoped it would be. In the meantime, Frankie was excitedly telling Tony that a fight had been scheduled. After that, maybe he'd quit. As the Petrocellis left, Tony sadly told Maggie, "You can cry for them, Maggie, but you can't live their lives for them." They both knew that Frankie would never willingly quit boxing.

COMMENTS: Don Stroud would be closely identified with *Mike Hammer* in the 1980s. He appeared in two Hammer films and the TV series.

Once Upon A Victim
Season 1: Episode 15
Aired Wednesday, January 29, 1975

Director: Herschel Daugherty
Writers: Leonard Katzman and Stanley Roberts
Producer: Leonard Katzman

GUEST STARS:
John Dehner (Dr. Leo Stegner)
Alan Fudge (Attorney Sam Markland)
Renne Jarrett (Lois Phillips)
Barbara Rhoades (Virginia Halima)
Jonathan Lippe (Dr. Gil Clayton)
Gene Earle (Herb Pipkin)
Della Reese (Angela Damon)
Fred Ashley (James Mantly, coroner)

STORYLINE: Dr. Gil Clayton drove his fiancée, Lois Phillips, home. They said good night, then she got out of the car and went into the house. Inside, she looked around for her mother, Rita Phillips, calling as she went from room to room. She found her in her bedroom on the floor, dead, with Dr. Leo Stegner kneeling by her with a scalpel in his hand. Angela Damond, head nurse at Dr. Stegner's clinic, told Tony that the doctor would have had no reason to murder Rita Phillips, the clinic's main source of support. Here's what Dr. Stegner told Tony: At 6:00 p.m., his assistant, Dr. Clayton gave him a telephone message from Rita Phillips that Dr. Stegner was to be at her house at exactly 10:30 that night. She was very demanding. He got there on time, let himself in with the key under the mat, and called out to her. There was no answer. He looked around for her and found her on the floor of her bedroom. He knew she was dead before he knelt down and checked her. He saw a scalpel on the floor and picked it up. Lois appeared in the doorway and began screaming, then ran off.

During the investigation of this case, Petrocelli was being followed by a sedan. Its driver kept shooting at him. The car chase got the attention of the police, who stopped Tony while the other car got away. When asked what that was all about, Tony told the police, "Any fish will bite if you give him the right bait." He knew he was on the right track.

SUBPLOT: In the Petrocelli office, another client, a politician, was upset that Tony wasn't able to find evidence of malpractice at a clinic. The politician wanted that doctor found guilty. Disgusted at his client's attitude, Tony gave him his retainer back and told him to leave. As the man was leaving in a huff, Maggie reached out and took the retainer from his hand, saying, "He's only the lawyer. I'm the bookkeeper. Thank you, Mr. Lathrop. Give our best to your constituents." Once he was gone, Maggie told Tony this was next month's trailer payment.

COMMENTS: Actor Jonathan Lippe is now known as Jonathan Goldsmith.

The Kidnapping
Season 1: Episode 16
Aired Wednesday, February 5, 1975

Director: Gunnar Hellström
Writer: Robert C. Dennis
Producer: Leonard Katzman

GUEST STARS:
Kim Darby (Donna McCaslin)
Patricia Blair (Angela Gilmartin)
Gene Evans (Senator Linville McCaslin)
Todd Lookinland (Jody McCaslin)
Fred Ashley (Mr. Bridger)
Arnold Jeffers (Judge)

STORYLINE: Senator McCaslin took grandson Jody to bed, then returned to the party downstairs. When Jody went into his room, a hand quickly covered his mouth. He turned around to see that the hand belonged to his mother, Donna McCaslin. They were so glad to see each other again! Pretending, for the child's sake, that they were playing a game, Donna kidnapped her son. The party guests were alerted that Jody had disappeared and his bedroom window was open, so they formed a search party outside to find him. Donna and Jody were running past the swimming pool when he stumbled. Donna stopped to be sure he was

Barry with guest star Kim Darby.

okay, but was interrupted by Angela Gilmartin, the senator's secretary, who sternly tried to stop them. Donna asked Angela to leave them alone, then told Jody to go to her car and she'd catch up with him. As he went off, she took Jody's bat and hit Angela in the stomach with it, just enough to knock the wind out of her so she couldn't follow them. Donna caught up with Jody and they went to her car. A man held the car door open for them, as mother and son got in and drove off. The search party arrived at the pool and found Angela floating in it, dead. Tony had to deal with a very powerful senator. The key witness was little Jody, but his mother refused to divulge where he was staying. It was Maggie who found him in a very clever way.

SUBPLOT: At the courthouse, Petrocelli pled for his client, Mr. Bridger, whose tool shed was partly on his neighbor's property. The judge told him to move the shed. "Ruling stands. Case dismissed." Tony had agreed to take his fee in bricks from the shed that had to be moved. They would be handy for home-building. Tony, Pete and Maggie went to Mr. Bridger's place to get their bricks. Tony took a sledgehammer and gave it a mighty swing, dislodging a brick. Mr. Bridger came out and said he decided to sell the building to his neighbor, Cliff.

"What about my fee?" Tony asked.

Mr. Bridger grinned. "If you forget about your fee, I won't tell Cliff what ya done to his building."

COMMENTS: Guest star Patricia Blair and *Petrocelli* regular Albert Salmi had been cast mates throughout the *Daniel Boone* TV series' 1964-65 season.

Wednesday, February 12, 1975 — Pre-empted

A Lonely Victim
Season 1: Episode 17
Aired Wednesday, February 19, 1975

Director: Irving J. Moore
Writer: Leonard Katzman
Producer: Leonard Katzman

GUEST STARS:
Anjanette Comer (Mary Thorpe)
Simon Scott (Ryder Carson)
Bobby Eilbacher (Billy Thorpe)
Mark Goddard (Perry Brooks)
Fred Beir (Raymond Walker)
Lowell Gleason (D.A. Bright)
Donald Dubbins (Joseph Bear)
Aram Chorbanian (Mark Briggs)
Madlyn Rhue (Ellen Walker)
Richard Elman (Dexter Tindle)
David Huddleston (Lt. Ponce)

STORYLINE: Neighborhood children were playing when young Billy Thorpe looked toward his apartment and saw that a stretcher carrying a body was being lifted into an ambulance and his mother, Mary Thorpe, was being led to a police car. He ran over to see what they were doing to her. She reassured him that she would be okay. Mary told Billy to go stay with his Uncle Joe until she got back. Lt. Ponce told one of the police officers to drive the boy to his uncle's house. A bit later, at the Petrocelli office, Tony was talking on the phone with Mama when Billy came in. The child said that Lt. Ponce drove him there and said that Mr. Petrocelli could help him. Billy told Tony that they had arrested his mother for killing her boss, Mr. Raymond Walker. Neighbors had seen her leaning over his body with the murder weapon in her hand.

SUBPLOT: A chatty stripper, Zazu O'Brien, from a previous small case was occasionally mentioned in this and other episodes. We chuckle over her continued troubles with the law.

COMMENTS: This is the first time we see Lt. Ponce's caring side.

The Outsiders
Season 1: Episode 18
Aired Wednesday, February 26, 1975

Director: Irving J. Moore
Writers: Leonard Katzman and Thomas L. Miller
Producer: Leonard Katzman

GUEST STARS:
Mitch Vogel (Ron Field)
Mark Hamill (David Mitchell)
Lucille Benson (Lucille Field)
William Bramley (Cyrus Mitchell)
Hayes Stewart (Andrew Sloan)
Charles Young (Paul Glass)
Marion Ross (Mary Sloan)
Gene Earle (Clyde Martin)

STORYLINE: There was a crash, then twenty-year-old Ron Field came out of the drugstore. Soon several men began chasing him. They finally caught him and police arrested him for breaking and entering. Lucille

Field came into the office and asked Petrocelli to help her son, but said they had no money. She said the police arrested her son Ron for murdering Mr. Sloan, who owned the drugstore, but Ron's a good boy. He would never hurt anyone. She said they're croppers, passing through town in a quest for work. Their truck had broken down and her husband's cough was getting worse, so Ron had gone into town to get him some cough syrup. How could the son in such a kind, humble family murder Mr. Sloan? Or did he?

SUBPLOT: Written into almost every episode was a loving scene. In this one, Tony was working at his desk when Maggie knelt down close to him and asked, *"Do you know what, Anthony J. Petrocelli?"*
"Uh-huh," he said absent-mindedly as he wrote notes in his file.
"What uh-huh?"
"You know what uh-huh."
"Tell me," she replied.
"Repeat the question, your honor."
"Do you know what, Anthony J. Petrocelli?"
"Yeah. You love me."
She chuckled and shook her head. *"We're having Texas style barbecue ribs tonight."*
"Texas style ribs, huh?"
"I invited the Fields over for dinner."
"That's nice, honey," he smiled.
"You know what?"
"What?"
"I love you."

COMMENTS: Mark Hamill would get his big break three years later in *Star Wars*.

Vengeance In White
Season 1: Episode 19
Aired Wednesday, March 5, 1975

Director: Leonard Katzman
Writer: Robert Stull
Producer: Leonard Katzman

GUEST STARS:
Michael Anderson, Jr. (Nathaniel Wakely)
Elinor Donahue (Joan Hiller)
Brenda Scott (Bonnie Wakely)
Michael Bell (Glenn Hiller)
Ken Swofford (Phillip Armor)
Francesca Jarvis (Aggie Crane)
Gene Earle (Ted Atchison)

STORYLINE: Evangelist Nathaniel Wakely was very effectively leading a tent revival gathering. Toward the end, he invited all to come forward to accept Jesus; and he and his hooded-robe-clad wife Bonnie went among the believers to greet them individually. Among the throng of people was Lt. Ponce, who arrested Bonnie right then and there for the murder of their manager, Phillip Armor. There had been an eye witness and the murder weapon had her fingerprints on it. Many people had grievances with the deceased, and several people were wearing the same kind of hooded robe. Who did it?

SUBPLOT: The theme this week was that money was tight for the Petrocellis. Tony and Maggie were busy painting their office, which would earn them free rent for a month. And later, Tony saw a parking meter officer coming near his camper. He went to the meter, took a coin out, and smiled at the officer, who then proceeded on to the next vehicle. Tony put the coin back in his pocket.

COMMENTS: Ken Swofford, formerly Petrocelli's detective in *The Lawyer*, returns in this episode and "Mark of Cain" as Lt. John Clifford, and as a completely different character in "Vengeance in White."

Four The Hard Way
Season 1: Episode 20
Aired Wednesday, March 12, 1975

Director: Joseph Pevney
Writer: William Kelley
Producer: Leonard Katzman

GUEST STARS:
Strother Martin (Clate Dobie)
Lina Raymond (Juno Tuttle)
Paul Brinegar (Patch Dressler)
John Crawford (Joe Tuttle)
Gloria LeRoy (Zazu O'Brien)

STORYLINE: Clate Dobie rushed into a western-style bar to tell his cowboy friends Patch, Toot, and Cy that he was on the run. He asked to borrow Patch's saddle. He said that he would be blamed for hurting Joe Tuttle, his daughter's husband, so the law was due to come down on him. It soon became more serious than that. Tuttle died. The cowboys pooled their meager money together and hired Petrocelli, their "good $25 lawyer," to defend Clate.

In order to talk to Clate, Tony was led on horseback to a remote location where Clate was hiding out. Saddle sore, Tony soon afterward walked painfully and stiffly to the courtroom to enter Clate's plea: Clate's "I never done it" was translated by his lawyer into "Not guilty, your Honor."

Evidence against him was strong. He was seen in the kitchen by the body with blood on his hands, the murder weapon was found in his saddlebag, Clate had written a farewell note to his daughter saying that if he stayed he'd end up killing Tuttle, and witnesses had seen him and Tuttle arguing earlier.

As Tony was mulling over the possibility that it had been Juno who killed Tuttle, Maggie couldn't imagine a wife murdering her husband. *Why?* Tony wondered. Because it's too risky. She said that Eve was a mere mortal who tempted Adam, but "it took all the wiles of the devil himself to tempt Eve."

Champagne glasses were the key pieces of evidence.

SUBPLOT: Stripper Zazu O'Brien was in the Petrocelli office, demonstrating her dance and strip act. Petrocelli told her to cut the lewdness out of her act, and the judge might let her go back to work.

After Clate's trial was over, Tony and Maggie were back at home. He was on the phone telling Zazu that he had warned her to take out the lewd parts of her act. He hung up and told Maggie that Zazu had been arrested again. An overzealous deputy had impounded her clothes as evidence, and she's "got a chill." He got up to go take care of it, and Maggie decided she'd better go, too. It wasn't Tony she didn't trust; it was Zazu. Before they could leave, Pete, Clate, and their buddies drove up. Pete said the men wanted to show their appreciation. They then presented Tony with a saddle of his own, and were seeing if they could get him a horse to go with it. The cowboys happily departed. Tony and Maggie quickly got into Pete's car, urging him to go now before those guys came back with a horse.

Zazu actress Gloria LeRoy.

COMMENTS: Zazu O'Brien's recurring character was delightfully quirky. She could provide comic relief to a tense episode.

Wednesday, March 19, 1975 — Pre-empted

Wednesday, March 26, 1975 — Pre-empted

Death In Small Doses
Season 1: Episode 21
Aired Thursday, March 27, 1975

Director: Don Taylor
Writers: Al Reynolds and John Dawson
Producer: Lou Morheim

GUEST STARS:
George O'Hanlon, Jr. (Lewis Baldwin)
Stephen Elliott (Martin Granger)
Elizabeth MacRae (Lucille Bates)
Robert Mandan (Sheriff Arnheit)
Torin Thatcher (George Baldwin)

STORYLINE: Lewis Baldwin found Lucille Bates, his grandfather George Baldwin's nurse, dead on the floor with a syringe in her neck. Scared, he ran. He was caught and charged with first-degree murder. The sheriff involved was extremely arrogant, and knew "the little punk" Lewis was the murderer, without benefit of evidence. Sheriff Arnheit, in fact, was the reason Pete Ritter had quit the police force and was now Tony's investigator.

In the process of building the case, Tony was shot at. The sheriff, of course, would not have the shooting investigated because it didn't serve his purposes.

We learn from the coroner about the difference between rigor mortis and livor mortis, which was crucial to solving the murder.

SUBPLOT: At the Petrocelli home site, Tony was sitting in what was intended to be the bathroom of their future house. He was annoyed that the toilet he ordered hadn't arrived yet. He showed Maggie where each room would be, including a nursery. The new toilet was delivered to the office the next day and Tony and Pete got to work assembling it. It was missing the flush valve! Pete and Maggie checked everywhere for a new flush valve, with no luck. Later, during the trial, Pete handed Tony a note. On it was a drawing of a toilet, with an arrow to the flush valve, and the words "Same as Arnheidt's office" on it.

After the trial was over, Petrocelli was in Sheriff Arnheidt's office, shaking hands with him and offering a truce. Pete came out of the restroom and shook his hand, too. After Tony and Pete left, Arnheidt heard a strange sound from that restroom and opened the door. His toilet was spewing water like a fountain.

As Pete and Tony happily left the building, Pete said, "One flush valve," and tossed it to Tony.

COMMENTS: Robert Mandan would soon break out of his bad-guy persona as *Soap* (1977-1981) comedy series regular, Chester Tate.

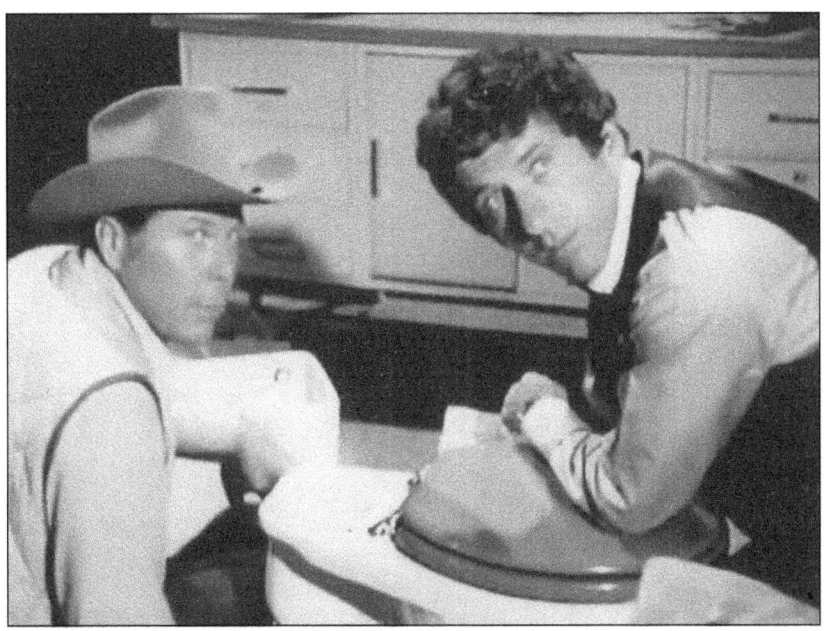

This page, previous: Screen captures from "Death in Small Doses."

A Night of Terror
Season 1: Episode 22
Aired Wednesday, April 2, 1975

Director: Bernard McEveety
Writer: William Kelley
Producer: Leonard Katzman

GUEST STARS:
Lois Nettleton (Gloria King)
Joseph Mell (Eric Frost)
Peter Mark Richman (Leo Roman)
Alan Fudge (Sam Murkland)
Morgan Woodward (Augie Briola)
Med Flory (Robert Miller)
Lance LeGault (Fred Kistler)

STORYLINE: Gloria King came to and found her abrasive gangster boyfriend Leo Roman dead on the floor beside her. She was arrested and charged with murder. A burglar who had been in the apartment at the time attested to her innocence, but the evidence was overwhelmingly against her. The murder weapon was in her hand, her fingerprints were the only ones on it, and she'd been receiving weekly checks from the mob for thirteen years.

Complicating matters was an explosion when Tony turned the ignition of his camper. It was small enough to simply serve as a warning, not to injure. The underworld didn't like to be questioned.

Was a hit man involved? Did she do the hit herself? Did the burglar do it?

SUBPLOT: A tiny one: Petrocelli was in the courtroom on another case and was surprised that the judge had asked him to set the sentence for his client — a lawyer's fondest dream. He said that a $100 fine would be fair. The judge said what he had in mind was a $50 fine. Tony commended the judge on his superior wisdom.

And another tiny subplot: When Tony returned to his office, Maggie was on the phone. She handed the phone to him and informed him that Zazu was still stripping and still being busted for it. He took the phone and talked to Zazu. Appearing shocked at something she said, he advised her to get attorney Armand V. Garcia to defend her. Maggie was dying of curiosity, but he wouldn't tell her what Zazu had done.

COMMENTS: Lois Nettleton, beginning as Miss Chicago in 1948, went on to become a Miss America semi-finalist in the same year. She and Peter Mark Richman had played a much more wholesome couple — Mary and Joseph — in the 1960 *Play of the Week* 'Emmanuel'.

Wednesday, April 9, 1975 — Pre-empted

Wednesday, April 16, 1975 — Pre-empted

"Hot enough for ya, guys?"

HALFTIME

Most of the time, the shows were filmed in Arizona; but a few times at the end of the season, interiors were shot at Paramount's studios in California.

As season one ended, it wasn't certain that there would be a season two for the show. There were plenty of reasons to continue it, however. Barry had been nominated for an Emmy as Outstanding Lead Actor in a Drama Series, and the show had many fans. Also, the editor of episode "Mirror, Mirror On the Wall" was awarded an Emmy for Outstanding Film Editing For Entertainment Programming for a Series. Finally, NBC announced in May that *Petrocelli* would be with us for another season on Monday nights at 10:00. It was changed back a month later to Wednesdays at 10:00 when the NBC schedulers learned that CBS would be running Anne Meara's show *Kate McShane*, a female attorney, at that same time. On ABC would be *Starsky and Hutch*, which would prove a very popular show. By mid-season, *Kate McShane* had been replaced by George Kennedy's police show *Blue Knight*, leaving *Petrocelli* the only surviving lawyer show.

Why had *Petrocelli's* renewal been iffy at all? As Barry told Bob Thomas, reported in *The Journal News* of White Plains, NY, "I couldn't understand that. If television is all about winning your time period, then there should have been no question about renewing us. The statistics are there. We started as the No. 3 show in our time period, pitted against two other new shows. Both of the others had high lead-ins — *Get Christie Love* had ABC's *Wednesday Movie of the Week* and *Manhunter* had *Cannon* preceding it. Our show had *Lucas Tanner*, which wasn't much help. Yet we managed to win our time period over the other two series, both of which were canceled. We managed to reach 34th in the ratings and had an audience share of 41 per cent last week."

Even columnist Earl Wilson noticed Barry's popularity. In his July 18, 1975 column, he wrote, "Barry Newman, who plays an attorney in the 'Petrocelli' TVer, got more mail than ever this season. 'But that's a false figure,' he [Newman] shrugs. 'Most of it was from people asking for free legal advice.'" Realistic acting, for sure.

It was not unusual for a new show to last only one season; that happened about 66% of the time. *Petrocelli* had fared better than its competitors during the first season, so was back stronger than ever. As *Bucks County [Pennsylvania] Currier Times* entertainment writer Lou Gaul

described its main character, "he's flashy in the legal arena, tough in the barroom, romantic in the bedroom, and fair in the judges' chambers. The delicate mixture of emotions and motivations works because of the stunning acting style of Barry Newman, who has the title role."

As a break during the August shooting for the second season, Barry and Susan flew back to Hollywood over a weekend to guest star on the

Barry guesting on Mike Douglas' show, with co-host Jackie Gleason.

nighttime version of *The Hollywood Squares*. He would often appear on Mike Douglas' show as well because he was such a witty guest.

Another outing happened on Sunday, October 12, 1975: "Petrocelli Night" at the Greyhound Park in Tucson. All three regulars of the show participated, along with Barry's date and Susan's husband, Calvin Chrane.

Petrocelli was being filmed for six months a year. Whenever he could, Barry would return to his beloved New York apartment. In Denise Kusel's column, for the article entitled "The 'Eyes of Texas' Are Upon Her," which ran in the *Independent Press-Telegram*, Susan told her, "The whole cast lives at the Hilton Hotel, and it's great. Sort of like going away to boarding school for six months and then back home for the other six months." Bedtime would have to be early when one is scheduled to begin work at 5:00 a.m., which they often were. Susan was happy that they were enlarging her role on the show so that she could help with the investigation. Maggie Petrocelli was such a likable lady that the fans were very glad that she would now be a larger part of the story.

Another change that would happen around the middle of the second season was that not every show would have a courtroom scene. There would be more action, less talk. Tony and Maggie's lives would be in jeopardy occasionally.

You may have noticed that Leonard Katzman was heavily involved in *Petrocelli* as producer, writer, and director. This series meant the world to him, and he was respected by those around him. Susan said, "I have always had a fondness and admiration for Leonard Katzman — a man of many talents. I found working with him to be a delight and he was always open to ideas and suggestions — he loved what he did and it showed."

The wildly-popular television series *Dallas* was Katzman's other baby. As *Dallas* star Larry Hagman wrote in his book *Hello, Darlin'*:

> "Then there was Leonard Katzman, the true genius behind the show. The man wrote, directed, produced, and served as the real head of the family. Without Leonard, Dallas wouldn't have been an eighth as successful. When I first met him in his office that day, I thought he was a real Hollywood producer, a kind of stereotype, and he turned out to be anything but that. He was a real human being, psychiatrist, rabbi, priest, ally, friend…and conniver. (Quoted with permission)

Death Ride
Season 2: Episode 1
Aired Wednesday, September 10, 1975

Director: Irving J. Moore
Writer: Katharyn Michaelian
Producer: Leonard Katzman

GUEST STARS:
Ned Beatty (Gage Hurley)
Ford Rainey (Hank Stevens)
Gerald McRaney (Cliff Rettiger)
John Crawford (Billy Elwood)
Diana Ewing (Dusty Stevens)
Don "Red" Barry (Vern)
Michael Bell (Frank Kaiser)
Gary Mike Casper (Harry)

STORYLINE: A rodeo was taking place, with brave riders on bucking bulls. Tony, Maggie, and Pete were in the bleachers, cheering for the rodeo clown, Pete's friend Gage Hurley. A cowboy was bucked off, and Gage humorously diverted the bull's attention away from the downed cowboy, who got back on his feet and hurried off to the side. Next up was the rodeo's star, Cliff Rettiger. After his few seconds atop the bull, he too met the ground and, a beat later, Gage came to his rescue. Once both men were back at the fence, Cliff accused Gage of being later than he should've been to distract the bull and that he did that on purpose. A fight between them ensued. As the announcer predicted over the loudspeaker, it was over quickly and the rodeo continued. Later, it would be learned that Gage had been arrested for killing Cliff. As Tony and Pete drove to the jail to talk to Gage, Pete filled him in on the details. Not only would it be difficult to defend Gage after thousands of people had seen them fighting earlier, but also because Gage had signed a confession! What Tony felt was a classic self-defense case, the prosecutor saw as murder-two because the victim was hit from behind.

COMMENTS: Ned Beatty's character, Gage, enjoyed being around children. Such seems to be the case with the actor, too: Within the group of excited children surrounding Ned in two scenes were Albert Salmi's younger daughters, Lizanne and Jenny. "I just remember having a blast at 'the rodeo'," says Lizanne. "I also remember swimming with Ned Beatty at the Hilton pool. He was a lot of fun and a very nice guy." Being the first episode of the second season, it was filmed during the summer, when school was out and Salmi's family was staying at the hotel with him.

This was the first of four episodes in which Michael Bell played prosecuting attorney Frank Kaiser. "Petrocelli was great fun to work on," he

Pete and his friend Gage.

says. "It was a test of an actor's ability to learn lines in a short time since the director liked long extended walking shots, so if you flubbed a line you had to do it all over again. I also had to take tennis lessons since Frank was somewhat of an expert and I had never played the game." Barry, who played tennis as much as he could in his off-screen time, probably enjoyed doing that tennis scene with Michael.

Mark of Cain
Season 2: Episode 2
Aired Wednesday, September 17, 1975

Director: Leonard Katzman
Writer: Leonard Katzman
Producer: Leonard Katzman

GUEST STARS:
John Saxon (Richie Martin)
Paul Koslo (Morgan)
Ken Swofford (Lt. John Clifford)
John H. Cox (Davis)

STORYLINE: Richie Martin's flight landed and he went from the tarmac into the airport, followed at a distance by two men. He went to the Petrocelli office. Tony wasn't in, so Richie chose to wait. Tony burst into the office with good news for Maggie — the case was dismissed. Richie came up behind him, and appeared to be pointing a gun in his pocket at Tony. He told Tony not to turn around, to drop the briefcase, and open the box he left on the desk. Tony slowly, cautiously opened the box. It was Mama's cannolis! Both men laughed and hugged. They had been childhood friends back in the old neighborhood in Boston.

The next evening, they were going to paint the town red together, but Richie wasn't at the hotel. He'd been arrested. Here's what he said happened: After a meeting the previous night, business associates Morgan and Davis offered to give him a ride back to the hotel. He was in the front passenger seat. They seemed to be going the wrong way. The car slowed down, Richie was hit on the back of his head, and a man walking out of a building was shot dead. The car went around the corner and crashed. When the police arrived and got him out of the car, Richie was groggy. The other two men were gone.

As Tony was leaving the building, Lt. Clifford approached him angrily, saying adamantly that he shouldn't take the case for such a low life as Richie Martin. He had a long rap sheet, was nothing but trash. The man he killed was a cop, Joe Thomas, shot most likely because he was doing underground work on the Mafia. Lt. Clifford had been told that Martin was coming to San Remo, so he had two men follow him from the airport. One followed him to Petrocelli's office and the other to a meeting with the southwestern head of the syndicate.

SUBPLOT: Bad guys Morgan and Davis kidnapped Maggie. That, they knew, was the only way they could get Petrocelli to betray Richie.

COMMENTS: This very intense episode didn't involve a courtroom scene. The focus was on the old chums' relationship and its very sad end. The relationship between Tony and Maggie was very deep, as was evidenced further in this episode.

When asked which episode was his favorite, Barry Newman's response was, "I like very, very much the one with John Saxon. He became a Mafia guy and I became a lawyer. [It was the episode] when my wife was kidnapped."

Barry with guest star John Saxon in his favorite episode.

Five Yards of Trouble
Season 2: Episode 3
Aired Wednesday, September 24, 1975

Director: Joseph Pevney
Writer: Williams Keys
Producer: Leonard Katzman

GUEST STARS:
Glenn Corbett (Charlie Royer)
Richard Jacome (Worham)
Barbara Luna (Dorothy Royer)
James J. Wiers (Pembro)
Robbie Rist (Ray)
Aram Chorebanian (Dr. Irwin Bliss)
H.M. Wynant (Ramsdale)
Steve Eastin (Martin Bossun)
Angela Clarke (Teresa Moran)
Arnold Jeffers (Judge)
Ron Foster (Alfred Woodward)

STORYLINE: A little-league baseball game had just been won by the team of Charlie Royer. Most of the team came off the field. Lagging behind was Charlie's nephew, Ray. Police arrived and arrested Charlie for the murder of Alfred Woodward. Seeing how upset that made Ray, Charlie told him to go tell Aunt Dorothy what happened, that it was all a mistake.

When Tony went to see him at the jail, here is what Charlie said happened: The previous afternoon, Ray had a game scheduled, so Charlie went first to pick Dorothy up at the club, her workplace, but she wasn't there. They said she had gone to Al Woodward's place. Charlie was angry about that because he'd almost gotten into a fight with Woodward earlier for coming on to Dorothy. When Charlie arrived at the man's house, Al was taking pictures of Dorothy in a bikini. Of course, that set Charlie off. He left, then returned with the cement-mixer truck and unloaded the wet cement into Woodward's convertible. The weight of the cement made the car collapse. Dorothy explained to Charlie that Al needed those pictures to submit to a person in Las Vegas. She wanted it to be a surprise for Charlie, that she'd get a high-paying waitress job at a Vegas gambling room and they could move there. Construction work for Charlie would be plentiful there. Charlie went back to the backyard, where Woodward had returned, to get the film out of his camera. Instead, he just threw the camera into the pool. A fight ensued. Woodward was on the ground. Charlie raised a golf club over his head, intending to deliver a mighty blow to Al with it. Before following through, though, he changed his mind because Al was already groggy. It was very unexpected that Charlie would later be arrested for Woodward's murder. He'd been alive when he last saw him.

SUBPLOT: At their house-in-progress, Maggie was watching Tony work on their patio-in-progress. All it needed, he said, was Maggie's handprints in the cement to make it official. They were then interrupted by Ray's entrance, asking Tony to defend his dad.

At the episode's end, Dorothy and Ray were throwing the ball to each other while Tony and Charlie finished laying the cement for the patio. Tony again wanted Maggie's handprints in it. As she put them in, the ball landed in the concrete, splattering Maggie. Tony laughed. Maggie threw a handful of cement at Tony.

COMMENTS: Like so many former child stars, Robbie Rist's creativity includes music. He's a composer and guitarist, while still keeping up with a busy acting schedule.

Shadow of Fear
Season 2: Episode 4
Aired Wednesday, October 1, 1975

Director: Irving J. Moore
Writer: Leonard Katzman
Producer: Leonard Katzman

GUEST STARS:
Anne Archer (Sherril Brewster)
William Windom (Alan Brewster)
Warren J. Kemmerling (Lt. Wayne Carter)
Victor Rendina (Apollo)
Jonathan Lippe (Harry Silver)
John Henry Cox (Tommy Archer)

STORYLINE: Sherril Brewster came to Petrocelli, asking him to go with her to turn herself in to the police because she had shot Tommy Archer, her first husband. He had come back into her life, intending to blackmail her. She didn't want her current husband, Alan, to know about her first marriage, so she went to his apartment and, in the darkened room, shot him.

In the meantime, her current husband was seen kneeling by the body, holding his gun and looking through the dead man's wallet. He was the one arrested for murder.

Who did it? Tommy was involved in the underworld, so maybe a hit man did it. The telling bit of evidence was a key.

SUBPLOT: This was Tony's penchant for betting on the horses, namely Armaghast, hoping that someday he'd strike it rich. The big race was being broadcast over the radio. Tony, Maggie, and Pete were gathered around, rooting for Armaghast as the excitement grew. It was a close race, and Armaghast won! Maggie and Pete were elated. They had both made bets on that horse. Tony was kicking himself. He had been so wrapped up in the case, he'd forgotten to bet.

COMMENTS: Anne Archer was a future star of the 1985 TV series *Falcon Crest*, created by Earl Hamner.

William Windom would play Commodore Decker in both the 1967 *Star Trek* TV series, and in the fan-producd *Star Trek: New Voyages* in 2004.

Barry and William Windom.

Chain of Command
Season 2: Episode 5
Aired Wednesday, October 8, 1975

Director: Herb Wallerstein
Writers: Katharyn Michaelian and Michael Michaelian
Producer: Leonard Katzman

GUEST STARS:
John Ritter (John Olson)
Warren Stevens (Gen. Drew)
Lee H. Montgomery (Freddie)
John Lupton (Billy Hanson)
Lin McCarthy (Leo Shane)
Kenneth Tobey (Jason Strafford)
Rosemary DeCamp (Mrs. Drew)
Francesca Jarvis (Mrs. Strafford)

STORYLINE: Airport mechanic John Olson, in leaving the airport, sped up and crashed through the guard's gate. The guard ran to the hangar to report the damage and found General Drew dead. Law enforcement caught up with Olson and arrested him for the murder. He verbally resisted arrest. Other evidence against him was that the General had fired him that day, his fingerprints were on the murder-weapon wrench, and he had been driving in the direction of Mexico when they apprehended him.

A Boy Scout named Freddie took the troop treasury's balance and went to see Petrocelli. Before hiring him to defend Scoutmaster Olson, Freddie asked Tony for his references, was impressed by them, and gave him the money as a retainer, saying the troop would raise the rest.

SUBPLOT: Maggie was having a terrible time trying to change the ribbon on her typewriter. Tony told her it just needed love and understanding, and gallantly stepped in to change it. He couldn't figure it out either. Boy Scouts to the rescue! Freddie fixed it, saying that it had been put in there upside down.

COMMENTS: Young Lee Montgomery, too, branched out into music later in life. He composed the soundtrack of *Legend of the Phantom Rider*, released in 2002.

Wednesday, October 15, 1975 — Pre-empted

Wednesday, October 22, 1975 — Pre-empted

To See No Evil
Season 2: Episode 6
Aired Wednesday, October 29, 1975

Director: Irving J. Moore
Writers: Leonard Katzman & Thomas L. Miller
Producer: Leonard Katzman

GUEST STARS:
Julie Kavner (Julie Carter)
Erica Hagen (Shirley Miller)
Michael Bell (Frank Kaiser)
Dave Hatunen (John Saffro)
Steve Sandor (Robert Jarvis)
Fred Ashley (Fred Nash)
Lee Allen (Buddy Landers)
Arnold Jeffers (Judge)

STORYLINE: Young people were frolicking in the apartments' pool when they heard two gunshots coming from Julie Carter's apartment. They ran to see what happened and discovered Buddy Landers dead on the floor at the foot of Julie's bed. Julie was in the bed, crying. She told Petrocelli that she had been sleeping, heard noises, took the gun from her nightstand and shot at the sound. She was blind, so couldn't see who she was shooting at. A simple case of self-defense? The prosecuting attorney wasn't convinced. Witnesses told him that Julie and Buddy had had a violent argument just an hour before the shooting. Because the prosecutor knew that Buddy was an undercover government agent, he thought that the argument was because she felt she was being used.

SUBPLOT: Fred Nash came to the Petrocelli homestead to inform them that the city council was seriously considering running the new highway through their property. The route would go through the house they were in the process of building. In a happy coincidence, Fred was a friend of Pete's. As a birthday present to Tony, Pete got the council to reroute the highway ten miles away from their property.

COMMENTS: In Mary O'Neill's November 3, 1975, "As I See It" column in the *Irving Daily News*, she wrote, "'Petrocelli' must have really startled a great many viewers the other night when 'Rhoda's' sister, Julie Kavner being her right name, gave a most astounding performance of a blind girl accused of murder.

"Throughout the entire program her eyes never seemed to waver — she just stared straight ahead as most blind people do. She was amazing."

Terror on Wheels
Season 2: Episode 7
Aired Wednesday, November 5, 1975

Director: Herb Wallerstein
Writer: Peter Lefcourt
Producer: Leonard Katzman

GUEST STARS:
John Colicos (Dimitri Petrakis)
Jim Antonio (Paul Wiggins)
Ayn Ruymen (Katie Petrakis)
Kipp Whitman (Nick Fenton)
Annette O'Toole (Tina Sullivan)
Paul Roland (Frank Jennings)
Gerald McRaney (Terry Santo)
Don Starr (Judge)

STORYLINE: Police rush into an apartment and find two men on the floor, one dead and one groggy. The dead man was Nick Fenton, motorcycle-gang boyfriend of the daughter of the other man, Dimitri Petrakis. Police took the gun away from Petrakis and arrested him. The now-prisoner tells Petrocelli that he had gone over to scare Fenton into leaving his daughter alone, not to kill him. He didn't kill him. Unfortunately for his defense, Petrakis had told people earlier that when he found Fenton, he'd kill him.

COMMENTS: While Gerald McRaney always seemed to play a bad guy on this series, he would go on to star in the 1989-1993 TV series *Major Dad*, and appear frequently in both *Touched by an Angel* (1985-1998) and *Promised Land* (1996-1999) as the very respectable Russell Greene.

The Gamblers
Season 2: Episode 8
Aired Wednesday, November 12, 1975

Director: Herb Wallerstein
Writer: John Hudock
Producer: Leonard Katzman

GUEST STARS:
A Martinez (Mando Rivera)
Jack Ging (James Wylie)
Mark Hamill (Dennis Wylie)
John Lupton (Billy Hanson)
Monika Ramirez (Teresa Rivera)
Charles Young (Joe Malone)
Eugene Kelly (Al Benton)

STORYLINE: A couple of his friends came looking for Al Benton at his pizzeria after it was closed and found him on the floor, stabbed to death. As they knelt down to him, Mando Rivera got up from behind the counter and ran out. Mando told Petrocelli that he worked for Benton, went back after hours to retrieve his textbook, and, because it was dark in there, tripped over his body. It didn't look good for seventeen-year-old Mando. The police officers noted the open cash register and, upon apprehending Mando, found money in his car that could have been stolen from it. Further investigation revealed Mando's fingerprints on the knife, and people who witnessed a violent argument between Mando and Benton earlier that day.

SUBPLOT: Mando had been taking care of his three younger siblings after their parents' death. He just *had* to be found innocent and released so the family wouldn't be broken up. Maggie and Tony looked in on them, helping when they could. Mando's younger sister Teresa was filling in for him while he was away.

COMMENTS: A Martinez went on to become hot property, being cast as a regular or semi-regular in many popular series, including *Santa Barbara, One Life to Live, L.A. Law, General Hospital,* and *One Life to Live.* From 2015 through 2017, he was a regular at the same time in *two* series: *Days of Our Lives* and *Longmire.*

Wednesday, November 19, 1975 — Pre-empted

Wednesday, November 26, 1975 — Pre-empted

Wednesday, December 3, 1975 — Pre-empted

Terror By The Book
Season 2: Episode 9
Aired Wednesday, December 10, 1975

Director: Irving J. Moore
Writer: Deena Silver-Kramer
Producer: Leonard Katzman

GUEST STARS:
Anne Francis (Emily Burke)
Marj Dusay (Eve Orland)
Dewey Martin (Bill Whitehead)
Michael Bell (Frank Kaiser)
Dick Butkus (Bill Eberly)
Ned Wilson (Roy Burke)
Bing Russell (John Miller)
S. John Launer (Max Franklin)

STORYLINE: Eve Orland and her friend Ellen drove up to the Orland house and were going inside for a drink when they heard a loud gunshot. Emily Burke then ran out of the house, got in her car, and swiftly drove away. Inside, Mark Orland was dead of a gunshot wound.

Emily told Petrocelli that Mark was an old friend and had called to ask her to come to his house for an interview for a book he was researching. This was the first time in years she would be seeing him, so she was looking forward to it. When she arrived, no one came to the door, so she went inside, calling his name. The gunshot rang out. Looking inside the den and seeing him dead, she got scared and ran.

Opposing attorney Frank Kaiser told Tony that witnesses had seen Emily and Mark in a restaurant the night before, arguing loudly. They heard her say that she'd kill him. Frank said that was because he'd written that she was a swinger in high school, and having that made public would hurt her marriage and her reputation.

SUBPLOT: Wexler Bottling Company, the provider of Tony's favorite root beer, was going out of business! Catastrophe! No other brand was as good as Wexler's. Maggie got Mr. Wexler on the phone for Tony, and they agreed to sell the Petrocellis the rest of their root beer stock at the wholesale price. He should've found out how many cases were left first. 530 cases, along with the invoice, were delivered and filled their trailer full.

COMMENTS: Anne Francis was known for her title role in the 1965-1966 TV series *Honey West*.

Face of Evil
Season 2: Episode 10
Aired Wednesday, December 17, 1975

Director: Irving J. Moore
Writer: Thomas L. Miller
Producer: Leonard Katzman

GUEST STARS:
Kay Lenz (Janet Wade/Mary Wade)
Robert F. Lyons (Sam Johnson)
Lucille Benson (Madge Briar)
Fred Beir (John Kelly)
Sandy Rosenthal (Dr. Koblin)
Fred Ashley (Henry Hoffler)
Henry Kendrick (Doc Simpson)
Shirley Poliakoff (Thelma)
Arnold Jeffers (Judge)
Norman Stone (Wallace)

STORYLINE: Madge Briar heard a noise from the other side of the hotel-room door, then saw Janet Wade run out and leave in haste. Looking into the room then, Madge saw Sam Johnson's body on the floor.
 Sexy Mary Wade came into the Petrocelli office and hired Tony to defend her sister Janet, who would be arrested that afternoon. Janet ("the mouse," as Mary called her) worked at the diner and would be easy to identify because she's her twin and looks just like Mary. Tony went to the diner and talked to Janet. Here's what she said happened: It began at 9:45 p.m. when a male customer came on to her. She gave him the

cold shoulder. He waited until her shift was over at 10:00 and said he'd take her home. She didn't remember how they got there, but said they were in a hotel room, she was on the bed, and her face was hurting. He attacked her, so she grabbed the first thing she could and hit him with it. In a daze, she went home. That's all she remembered. She didn't realize that he had died from that blow.

It's hard to believe that Kay Lenz could ever look like a shy 'mouse', isn't it, but she absolutely pulled it off.

"Is this the same story you told your sister?" Tony asked.

"Sister? Mr. Petrocelli, I don't have a sister."

Really confused now, Tony asked, "Is Mary Wade your sister?"

Understanding now, she responded, "Let's just say that we have the same mother and father."

This case got stranger and stranger. DA John Kelly later told Tony that eye witnesses in the diner said Janet made a play for Sam. She flirted with him and asked him to drive her home. It was she who was the aggressor, not he. A witness in the hotel heard her ask him for money, and that's when the struggle began.

SUBPLOT: There were two subplots:

Pete was at a farm, helping hold the sheep still while the veterinarian gave them vaccinations, when Tony went to talk to him about the case. Sheep all finished, the doctor then asked Pete to get the goat for him. Pete chased that animal around, but couldn't catch him. Maggie caught him with a lasso.

When Tony went to question Madge, she was outside, painting. He politely complimented her artwork so, in gratitude, she gave him one of her seascapes. Tony put it in the camper and forgot about it until later, when Maggie gave him an anniversary present. Having completely forgotten their anniversary, he bluffed a bit. He went to the camper, got the painting, and said he just didn't have time to wrap it. Her response to the painting matched his. "It sure is blue," she said.

COMMENTS: *Warning: Spoiler Alert!* Kay Lenz's acting in this episode was awesome as she transformed herself from the shy, frightened sister to the outgoing, party-girl sister. In one continuous take, her posture, attitude, eye contact, voice, speech patterns, volume, intensity, facial expression, and self-assuredness changed. Undoing her pony-tail and pulling her hair forward completed the transformation. It was amazing to watch.

Too Many Alibis
Season 2: Episode 11
Aired Wednesday, December 24, 1975

Director: Herb Wallerstein
Writer: Fred Freiberger
Producer: Leonard Katzman

GUEST STARS:
Robert Hooks (Dr. Dave Hill)
Bettye Ackerman (Ann Hendricks)
Susan Sullivan (Janet Wilson)
Gloria Calomee (Cobbie Hill)
Sally Kirkland (Joan Arnold)
Gino Ardito (Mr. Thomas)
Marian Gibson (Emma Nolan)
Riley Hill (Allen Mitchell)
Arnold Jeffers (Judge)
Steve Eastin (Detective Brock)

STORYLINE: Maggie was driving when the brakes on a child's bicycle failed and he veered in front of her car. She swerved to avoid hitting him and he went down the hill. When Maggie got to him, he was unconscious, so she picked him up and took him to the hospital. Dr. Hill, a very kind and compassionate resident with a great bedside manner, took care of him. Officers came in and arrested him for the murder of Dr. Wilbur Hendricks. The two doctors had frequently argued, Dr. Hill's fingerprints were all over the murder weapon (a scalpel), and a waiter had heard Dr. Hill tell his wife that he'd kill Dr. Hendricks if he didn't leave him alone.

SUBPLOT: Viewers got a chuckle when Petrocelli went to question Mrs. Hill, a nurse who was in the process of administering flu shots to children. The child in front of her resisted the inoculation, but agreed to take a shot if the man did. So, Tony had to endure a flu shot in order to get the answers he was seeking.

COMMENTS: Fans of police shows know Robert Hooks from his Detective Jeff Ward role on *N.Y.P.D.* for the entire run of the show (1967-1979).

A Deadly Vow
Season 2: Episode 12
Aired Wednesday, December 31, 1975

Director: Irving J. Moore
Writer: Leonard Katzman
Producer: Leonard Katzman

GUEST STARS:
Rosemary Forsyth (Lauren Edwards)
Warren Kemmerling (Lt. Wayne Carter)
Davey Davison (Ginny Morgan)
Salome Jens (Leah Barnes)
Alan Landers (Jeff Morgan)
Len Wayland (Jack Mayhew)
Arnold Jeffers (Judge)
Sandy Rosenthal (Goldie)
Steve Eastin (Mr. Eastin)
Stephen Blood (Allan Edwards)
Paul Roland (Thomas Welch)

STORYLINE: Lauren Edwards came into the Petrocelli office and asked what would happen to a person who committed murder, and what would happen to the killer's child? Tony explained the different types of murder — involuntary, heat of the moment, etc. — and the corresponding levels of punishment. Why was she asking? She said she was going to kill her husband.

Soon afterward, her dead husband was removed from his house and Lauren was arrested. She swore to Tony that she didn't do it. She said she was going to, then realized she couldn't go through with it. Evidence against her: she indicated intent beforehand, she bought the murder weapon that day, her fingerprints were on the gun's grip, and motive: her husband had raped her sister.

SUBPLOT: Tony, another lawyer, and two doctors were in race cars, having a friendly contest. Tony came in second. He asked race car owner Goldie what he owed him for use of his car. He said he'll put it on the tab. The condition of that tab? So far, he owed Goldie two divorces, a will, and a simple assault. Pete enjoyed racing, too, so Maggie thought she'd give it a try on Ladies' Day. Tony wasn't sure he liked that idea.

COMMENTS: The racing scene was filmed at the Corona Speedway. It brought to mind Barry Newman's starring role in the film *Vanishing Point*.

Wednesday, January 7, 1976 — Pre-empted

Wednesday, January 14, 1976 — Pre-empted

The Falling Star
Season 2: Episode 13
Aired Wednesday, January 21, 1976

Director: Russ Mayberry
Writer: Leonard Katzman
Producer: Leonard Katzman

GUEST STARS:
Ken Curtis (Harry Underwood)
Frank Aletter (Lee Larker)
Susan Dey (Jenny Halliday)
George Petrie (Mannie Tyler)
Francine York (Lisa Farley)
Lawrence Casey (Buddy Vanders)
Nobel Willingham (Artie Jacobs)
Suzanne Zenor (Gigi Laverne)
Ron Foster (Sgt. Gilliam)
Arnold Jeffers (Judge Maitland)

STORYLINE: Harry Underwood was among those watching the shooting of a movie on a street in San Remo. Tony, Maggie, and Pete were there, too. Pete introduced Tony and Maggie to his friend Harry. It dawned on Tony who Harry was — Dusty Rhodes, the cowboy hero whose movies he had watched as a child in Boston.

Later, Pete came to Tony in distress. They had arrested Harry for the murder of Mannie Tyler, the film producer. Harry said he didn't do it. He went to the hotel bar to see Mannie to reminisce about old times, but saw he was talking to some people, so he sat at a table and waited, having a couple drinks during that time. Then Mannie left, so Harry finished his newly-poured third drink, then went to Mannie's room. He knocked on the door, which then opened. It was dark inside, but Harry went in, calling for Mannie. He then tripped over something — Mannie's dying body, with a letter opener protruding from his chest. Harry pulled the letter opener out. Having heard the din created by Harry's tripping, people came in to see what had happened. What they saw was Harry kneeling over Mannie with the murder weapon in his hand.

Evidence against him: the eye witnesses after the stabbing had happened, Harry's fingerprints on the letter opener, and two motives: 1) Harry's estranged daughter had received unwanted advances in the bar by Mannie, and 2) Mannie, back in Harry's Hollywood days, had been his business manager, who invested and lost over a million of Harry's dollars.

SUBPLOT: Former client GiGi Laverne came into the Petrocelli office to tell Tony that she had followed his advice and taken the bumps and grinds out of her act, so she shouldn't get arrested anymore. Tony wasn't there, but GiGi was happy to show Maggie how to do the bumps like a pro. Maggie caught on quickly.

COMMENTS: Might Zazu O'Brien have been originally intended for this episode but, perhaps, the actress (Gloria LeRoy) had other commitments, so another beautiful actress with a different stripper-character name filled in? If so, they must have liked her because GiGi would be back a few episodes later.

Survival
Season 2: Episode 14
Aired Wednesday, January 28, 1976

Director: Art Fisher
Writer: Leonard Katzman
Producer: Leonard Katzman

GUEST STARS:
Cindy Williams (Carol Janssen)
Jonathan Lippe (Paul Morgan)
Christopher Connelly (Don Janssen)
René Enriquez (Sgt. Hank Morales)
Moe Mosley (Moe)

STORYLINE: A burglar in a ski mask went in the window of the Moran office and robbed the safe. The night watchman came in and was knocked unconscious with the burglar's flashlight. The burglar then heard other officers coming and fled. As he rushed out of the parking garage, he barely missed hitting the attendant, who took note of his car tag's number.

Evidence against Don Janssen: He's an escaped prisoner, was caught in Santa Rosita on his way to Mexico, and they found the ski mask in his car.

Left: Don Janssen and Tony being hunted down in the desert.
Right: 'Survival' says it all.

SUBPLOT: A major one: Tony went to Santa Rosita to talk to Don, and they let Tony ride along when they were driving him back where he belonged. On the way, a man who wanted the contents of the safe (Paul Morgan) shot their driver, causing their vehicle to tumble down the hill. Tony and Don escaped the car right before Morgan shot it and it burst into flames. With no cell phones available, there was no way to let Maggie or the police know what was happening as Tony and Don fought for survival while being pursued by a gunman in desert conditions, getting injured along the way. Maggie and Pete were, of course, very worried when Tony didn't return as expected.

COMMENTS: The acting in Susan Howard's scene in which Maggie was talking to Mama on the phone, all the while being worried sick about Tony, was outstanding. She was trying so hard to keep Mama from fretting, but could barely hold back the tears herself.

The Night Visitor
Season 2: Episode 15
Aired Wednesday, February 4, 1976

Director: Robert Sheerer
Writer: Leonard Katzman
Producer: Leonard Katzman

GUEST STARS:
Joan Van Ark (Chris Parker)
Ken Swofford (Lt. John Clifford)
Phillip Pine (Ed Parker)
Thayer David (Arnold MacIver)
Moe Mosley (Moe)
Ray Cardi (policeman)

STORYLINE: Ed Parker was being followed by threatening-looking men one night, saw that the Petrocelli office light was on, and went there. Tony wasn't in, so he used the lawyer's phone to make a call, wrote a note and put it into an envelope, then asked Maggie to hold the envelope for him until he returned the next day. He left. When Tony and Maggie got to the office the next morning, it had been trashed. Chris Parker came in, asking for the "thing" that her father had left there. She couldn't describe it. They didn't give her anything. Tony went to see Ed Parker and found his place trashed, too, and Ed murdered. Immediately, police arrived and arrested Tony for the murder. Lt. Clifford knew Tony was not guilty, so set him free.

Arnold McIver came to Tony, wanting the envelope. He said it was his, giving a clue to where his property is. He said Chris killed Ed and wasn't really Ed's daughter.

Both Chris and Arnold claimed different names as the story progressed. Who were they really? Who committed the murder? And why?

SUBPLOT: McIver and his thugs kidnapped Maggie.

COMMENTS: Thayer David is remembered for his various roles (Mordecai Grimes, Ben and Prof. Timothy Stokes, Matthew Morgan, and Count Petofi, usually) throughout the run of *Dark Shadows* (1966-1971).

Ray Cardi went on to produce the 1979 film *The Sweet Creek County War*, in which Albert Salmi played the second lead.

Blood Money
Season 2: Episode 16
Aired Wednesday, February 11, 1976

Director: Irving J. Moore
Writer: Norman Lessing
Producer: Leonard Katzman

GUEST STARS:
Denver Pyle (Andrew Warburton)
Nicholas Hammond (Whitey)
James Daughton (Andy Warburton, III)
Andrew Rubin ("Doc" Holliday)
David Huddleston (Lt. John Ponce)
Suzanne Zenor (Gigi Laverne)
James Gammon (Harry)
Timothy Scott (Gus)
Darrell Larson (Al)
Don Starr (Judge)

STORYLINE: During a frat party in full bloom, two men in masks came in and took Andy Warburton with them at gunpoint. It was a kidnapping, and they soon sent a ransom note: if they didn't receive $500, they would shave Andy bald. This was just a prank, to get back at the fraternity for some vandalism they'd done. When Tony went to deliver the $500, the kidnappers had been roughed up and Andy was gone. He was *really* kidnapped. They wanted Maggie to deliver the much-larger ransom. When Andy's grandfather, Mr. Warburton, gave the Petrocellis that information, Tony said no. Mr. Warburton said no. Maggie said yes. She wanted to help free Andy, an old family friend. The men agreed only if Tony went with her.

Lt. Ponce somehow got wind of the kidnapping and, knowing that Mr. Warburton didn't want the police involved, offered to give his help unofficially. He set up a bugging system. When Tony and Maggie went to deliver the money, Ponce and Pete were nearby. While Tony was at the pay phone, a previously-unseen kidnapper took off in the camper with Maggie, so now she was kidnapped, too.

SUBPLOT: One of the early scenes provided some comic relief to an otherwise very serious episode. Gigi Laverne was on trial for lewd dancing, and Tony was defending her. She explained that all was fine until her trained dove went off-script and pulled all her fans off, leaving her nude. She demonstrated her dance to a very interested court, and it was deemed not lewd by the smiling judge.

COMMENTS: Denver Pyle seemed to be all over the place on TV and in movies, but his most-remembered role would be that of Uncle Jesse in *The Dukes of Hazzard* 1979-1985.

Left: Andy has been kidnapped! *Right:* It's his grandfather's money they want.

Any Number Can Die
Season 2: Episode 17
Aired Wednesday, February 18, 1976

Director: Leonard Katzman
Writer: Jeff Myrow and Leonard Katzman
Producer: Leonard Katzman

GUEST STARS:
Paul Burke (John Flemming)
Joshua Bryant (Paul Andrews)
Mark Gordon (Frank Keegan)
Gwynne Gilford (Jean Andrews)
David Huddleston (John Ponce)
Francesca Jarvis (Joan McCarthy)
Steve Eastin (Bob Gerber)

STORYLINE: After Paul Andrews' employee was deliberately hit by a car and killed, he came into the Petrocelli office to have his will made out. He also gave Tony a large envelope addressed to Frank Keegan, and asked that it be stipulated in the will that only Keegan was to get it. Tony took the finalized will to Andrews' store the next night and had

Left: David Huddleston as Lt. Ponce. *Right:* Steve Eastin, a familiar face in seven episodes. PHOTO COURTESY OF STEVE EASTIN

him sign it before his employee-witnesses, after which Andrews told his employees to take the rest of the day off. They left, and so did Tony. The store suddenly burst into flames, killing Andrews. A few days later, Tony agreed to meet Frank Keegan at his hotel so he could give him the envelope. When he got there, there had been an elevator accident, killing Keegan.

Maggie with Flemming. Was he really a government agent or someone more sinister?

Now government agent John Flemming wanted the envelope. Is he a good guy or a bad one? Who could Tony and Maggie trust? Who's doing all the killing?

SUBPLOT: To be closely associated with this feisty lawyer is no walk in the park. Maggie got roughed up by a baddie. Not content to stop there, the bad guy also took Pete hostage.

COMMENTS: Paul Burke was regular character Detective Adam Flint in the *Naked City* TV series of the early 1960s. Later that same decade, he was Colonel Joe Gallagher in *12 O'Clock High*. He would go on to be very present in the *Santa Barbara* and *Dynasty* series of the 1980s.

Six Strings of Guilt
Season 2: Episode 18
Aired Wednesday, February 25, 1976

Director: Don Weis
Writer: John Hudock
Producer: Leonard Katzman

GUEST STARS:
Joanna Miles (Sally Barnes)
Wayne Tippit (Det. Will Lewis)
Ward Costello (Thomas Barnes)
Martin Kove (Frank Harris)
Tammy Harrington (Judy Barnes)
Claire Brennen (Georgia)
Moe Mosley (Moe)
Franklin Brown (Leo Miles)

Claire Brennen, E. Jack Neumann, and Barry Newman. What the bartender wouldn't tell Petrocelli, dancer Georgia would.
PHOTO COURTESY OF MRS. E. JACK NEUMAN

STORYLINE: Pete's waitress lady-friend, Sally Barnes, was a widow with a young daughter named Judy. Because Sally worked and dated, her father-in-law petitioned the court for custody of Judy, thinking he and his wife could give the child a better life. A rejected boyfriend, Leo Miles, threatened Sally that, if she didn't give him money, he would testify against her in the custody trial. She gave him all she had — $600.

After a date with Sally, Pete was getting ready to drive away when he was arrested for the murder of Leo Miles. True, Sally had told him about Leo's blackmailing her and, furious about it, he had gone to his motel, but he didn't think he had killed him. Rather, Leo was coming at him, so Pete hit him a couple of times, leaving Leo on the floor. It was purely self-defense.

Of course, Tony and Maggie wanted to take out a bank loan to bail Pete out, and Tony did everything he could to prove Pete's innocence, but how do you prove self-defense when there were no witnesses? Bartenders were no help — they never recognize pictures of their customers.

COMMENTS: *Petrocelli* creator E. Jack Neuman made a cameo appearance in one scene as the bartender.

Deadly Journey
Season 2: Episode 19
Aired Wednesday, March 3, 1976

Director: Paul Lynch
Writer: Donnell-Di Maggio
Producer: Leonard Katzman

GUEST STARS:
Lucille Benson (Lucille Davis)
Marion Ross (Janet Williamson)
Alan Vint (Joe Davis)
Lynn Borden (Susan Kurry)

STORYLINE: Tony and Pete picked up an unusual hitchhiker — Lucille Davis, a friendly, down-home lady who was on her way to California, by way of San Remo. She was going to drop by her son's business to visit for a bit before continuing her trip. They dropped her off at San Remo Motors and went on their way.

When Pete was later in the police station, he saw them bring Lucille in in handcuffs. She'd been arrested for the murder of her son's boss, Mr. Williamson. What happened: After finding out that Williamson had mistreated her son, Lucille went back to San Remo Motors to give Williamson a piece of her mind. It was dark. She went into the dark building, heard a gunshot, and ran toward the sound, with the intent to help if someone was injured. She tripped over something, dropping her purse. When she knelt down to retrieve her purse, what she picked up was a gun. At that moment, the night watchman turned on the light and saw her by the body of the now-dead boss with the murder weapon in her hand. We all knew that sweet Lucille wasn't the murderer, but who was? Plenty of people had motive and/or opportunity — the uncooperative business partner, the hothead husband of Williamson's girlfriend Susan, Williamson's dying wife, even the night watchman. The cab driver who had taken Lucille back to San Remo Motors told the police that she had said Williamson would never mistreat anyone again.

SUBPLOT: One brief scene turned into a comedy of sorts. When Tony went to Susan's house to question her, her belligerent husband asked her who he was. Covering up her affair with Williamson, she said Tony was a salesman. Tony then went into a fast-talking, salesman-like spiel and urged them to fill out a household products questionnaire, which would take only about an hour to do. Of course, the husband told him to go away and shut the door.

COMMENTS: Who could blame Lucille Benson for being such a favorite of the casting director? This was the fourth character she played on *Petrocelli*.

The Pay Off
Season 2: Episode 20
Unaired

Director: Joseph Pevney
Writer: Mann Rubin
Producer: Leonard Katzman

GUEST STARS:
Victor French (Roy Caldwell)
Dabney Coleman (Willy Morgan)
Joanna Moore (Kay Willis)
Donny Most (Will Johnson)
Linda Dano (Lila Danford)
Whit Bissell (Douglas Johnson)
Burr DeBenning (Vince Belmont)
Mark Goddard (Bo Keller)
Don Starr (Judge)

STORYLINE: The Petrocellis welcomed Maggie's Uncle Roy at the airport. Before he could join them for the bountiful meal she'd planned, he had to go to a meeting that lasted until very late that night, so they drove him to his hotel. They were awakened by a call, saying that Roy had been arrested for the murder of a woman. Here's what he said happened: Roy was having a drink at the hotel bar, struck up a conversation with an attractive lady who was also from Tyler, Texas. Her name was Lila Danford. At closing time, they went to her room for another drink. They walked in and he was hit from behind, dropping unconscious onto the bed. As he was coming to, he heard a scream, then Lila fell on the bed beside him. He saw a blurred flash of light, and heard a door slam. Soon after, the desk clerk knocked on the door to see if Lila was all right. There was no response, so he opened the door. A crowd gathered around him, so he left and called the police. In the meantime, his father, who owned the hotel, stayed with Lila and Roy until the police arrived.

Lila was a prostitute and the "flash of light" was her photographer accomplice, whose pictures allowed her to blackmail her customers. The photo of Roy showed him on the bed, leaning over her dead body. The bartender had seen Roy and Lila drinking together, then going to her room. No one saw anyone else come or go from that room.

SUBPLOT: In their rush to get to the airport on time, Tony parked in front of the door (a no-parking area) and lifted the hood before rushing inside. The car was impounded. It took him the whole episode to find it and get it back. In the meantime, he was taking cabs and using Pete's car to get around.

COMMENTS: Not only would Victor French play regular roles on *Little House on the Prairie* and *Highway to Heaven* in later years, but he also directed many of their episodes, as well as the final episode of *Petrocelli*, "Jubilee Jones."

Shadow of A Doubt
Season 2: Episode 21
Unaired

Director: Jerry London
Writer: Sean Forestal
Producer: Leonard Katzman

GUEST STARS:
Harold Gould (Haskell Fox)
Brian Libby (James Buck)
Katherine Helmond (Nancy Berwick)
Tim Matheson (Mike Fisher)
William Prince (Judge David Anderson)

STORYLINE: Nancy Berwick was walking down the street when she heard a loud alarm go off. She looked in the window of a business and saw James Buck leaning over a dying man. James looked around, saw her, and ran out of the building, past her. Prosecuting attorney "Foxy" said he had motive, the murder weapon, and an eyewitness. Here's what James said happened: He had had some construction work done, then lost his job. Shortly afterward, the bill for the construction work had been sent to a collection agency that kept adding more charges to it. He went to talk to them about it, hoping to work something out. No one seemed to be there until he tripped over the dying man, who reached over and set off the alarm.

SUBPLOT: Tony was removed from the case and suspended when Mrs. Berwick accused him of trying to bribe her to change her testimony. Foxy, being a friend of Tony's, knew he was innocent, but had to conduct the investigation anyway. If found guilty, Tony could go to jail for up to seven years and be disbarred. Maggie and Pete did everything they could to help. A young attorney, Mike Fisher, replaced Tony on the case, and they worked together on it.

COMMENTS: Tim Matheson (Mike Fisher) has had an amazing career beginning in his childhood and is still going strong today. He has a long list of credits as a director, as well.

Jubilee Jones
Season 2: Episode 22
Unaired

Director: Victor French
Writer: John Hudock
Producer: Leonard Katzman

GUEST STARS:
Scatman Crothers (Jubilee Jones)
Michael Bell (Frank Kaiser)
Beah Richards (Bessie Jones)
Mary-Nancy Burnett (Sandra Simms)
Barbara Rhoades (Shirley Peters)
Dick Wesson (Frankie Welsh)
Sheldon Allman (Phil Kingsley)

STORYLINE: At the Starlight Club, Jubilee Jones was arrested for murdering the manager, Ed Harris. He said he was singing and dancing to a welcoming audience, then finished and went offstage. Reporter Sandra Simms asked him if being onstage reminded him of the good old days. He then went to Harris' office, turned on the light, and discovered the man dead on the floor. They'd had an argument earlier that evening because Harris took an *un*agreed-upon cut from his paycheck, and he'd hit the manager. That, he felt, made it look like he'd been the one to murder him, but he wasn't. Investigation turned up three other performers who had argued with Harris, too.

A critical piece of evidence was voice prints.

SUBPLOT: During the investigation phase, Tony went into the seemingly empty Starlight Club and began doing a dance. When Frankie Welsh showed up, they jokingly did James Cagney impressions to each other.

How was Tony's impression? Not so great, admitted Welsh. That was all right, Tony said, because he's really a dancer.

COMMENTS: In his later years, Scatman Crothers' distinctive voice would often be called on to do voice work, as well as straight acting. He was also a fine musician.

...AND THEN

In spite of the fact that Barry Newman, Susan Howard, and the series itself were all nominated for the Golden Globe Award in 1976...

Even though Susan Howard was nominated for the Primetime Emmy Award for Outstanding Continuing Performance by a Supporting Actress in a Drama Series in 1976...

Not to mention director Leonard Katzman's Edgar Allan Poe Award nomination for Best Television Episode ("Mark of Cain") in 1976...

Or that the show had made the covers of numerous magazines...

...1976 was the year *Petrocelli* was cancelled. Not logical, for sure, but as they say, "That's show biz."

Thank you, Tony and Maggie, for being such fine role models.

CRITICS' CORNER

SEPTEMBER 11, 1974 — *Washington DC Star News, Judy Flander:* "It's always been my theory that if television producers could come up with a solid unpredictable plot, professional acting and real people with believable lines, they'd have a TV show that would rival any first-class movie. Now, along comes NBC's 'Petrocelli,' which premieres tonight at 10 on WRC-4, which proves the theory."

SEPTEMBER 15, 1974 — *Hutchison Kansas News:* "There are several gimmicks here…Petrocelli (pronounced Petrochelli) is an Italian-American Phi Beta Kappa graduate of the Harvard Law School. He has settled in a 'southwest cattle town' to defend the oppressed and protect the public virtue. His courtroom tactics are unconventional but his dress is partial to vested suits, although not without touch of flair to the cut."

SEPTEMBER 17, 1974 — *The Courier-Journal* [Louisville, KY] Quoting Barbara Zuanich of *The Los Angeles Herald-Examiner:* "Functions at optimum pitch. It holds your attention and concentration throughout the hour. The premier script…is without a flaw, and the story is devoid of the usual whodunit clichés."

OCTOBER 9, 1974 — *The Kansas City Times, Joyce Wagner:* "The key to Petrocelli's success lies in the performance of its star, Barry Newman. He is an exciting actor, with a freshness and verve not often found within the sterile confines of the television school of acting."

OCTOBER 30, 1974 — *The Pittsburgh Press, Jerry Buck, Associated Press:* "Newman is in the tradition of Humphrey Bogart, James Cagney and Spencer Tracy."

Paramount Television release, by Rex Polier: Not since Peter Falk bowed in *Columbo* has TV had a star and series capable of creating as much excitement and entertainment as actor Barry Newman does in *Petrocelli*.

And this one is so perfect that it deserves repeating:

As the *Bucks County Currier Times* entertainment writer Lou Gaul described Tony Petrocelli, "he's flashy in the legal arena, tough in the barroom, romantic in the bedroom, and fair in the judges' chambers. The delicate mixture of emotions and motivations works because of the stunning acting style of Barry Newman, who has the title role."

GOLDEN NUGGETS

In Marilyn Beck's gossip column of Florida Today, *November 20, 1974:*
"Barry Newman was hauled into court the other day. Not to film a scene for his NBC 'Petrocelli' series…but to testify in a murder trial. Barry says the show's Paramount-TV cameras were filming at the entrance of Tucson's Pima County Courthouse when he was slapped with a subpoena to appear at the trial in progress inside. Seems the attorney for the defense made a plea for a mistrial after he noticed three women jurors talking to Newman during the lunch break. The plea was dismissed when Barry swore under oath that the ladies had merely asked him for autographs — and that he had merely been kidding when he told them 'If the defendant needs a good lawyer, tell him to look me up.'"

In Dorothy Manners' column in The Boston Herald American, *March 14, 1975:*
"…Barry Newman (star of the 'Petrocelli' TV series in which he plays a lawyer), said on being introduced by F. Lee Bailey at a luncheon in New York: 'Playing a lawyer and being introduced by Mr. Bailey makes me feel like the lead in a grammar school play being introduced by Laurence Olivier.'"

In Elaine Raines' article in The Arizona Daily Star, *December 17, 2008:*
"During the filming of one segment, in August, 1974, the script called for a car to pull up to the sidewalk near the Southern Arizona Bank. The driver got out and walked away. It just so happened a Tucson policeman was in the area and he walked right into the scene to write up a parking ticket. CUT!

"The film company had received permission to use the curb and street for their filming. Word had apparently not been passed down to the officers."
    and
"In 1975, the script called for a nighttime cemetery shootout. Passersby called to report the commotion at Southlawn Cemetery on S. Park Ave."

TRIVIA

1. What nationality was Anthony J. Petrocelli's proud heritage?

2. Which semi-regular character liked to tease Tony by mispronouncing his surname?

3. What did Mama Petrocelli look like?

4. What are Tony's and Maggie's hometowns?

5. When did Tony and Maggie meet?

6. Besides Barry Newman, Susan Howard, and Albert Salmi, which actor appeared on the show most often?

7. Which film clip shown at the beginning of each show doesn't come from the TV series?

8. What's the name of Tony's stripper-client?

9. How many bricks each day did Tony lay when building their house?

10. With what Italian phrase did Tony always end his phone conversations with Mama?

ANSWERS

1. *Italian.*

2. *Lt. Ponce.*

3. *We don't know. We never saw her.*

4. *The same as the actor's and actress' — Barry and Tony are from Boston, Massachusetts; Susan and Maggie are from Marshall, Texas.*

5. *When they were in college.*

6. *Arnold Jeffers, as the judge on 15 episodes. Fellow judge Don Starr came a close second, logging in at 14 episodes.*

7. *The woman's hand reaching down to touch the man's hand. That's Diana Muldaur's hand, from a scene in the film* The Lawyer.

8. *There were two of them: Zazu O'Brien in 1975 and GiGi Laverne in 1976.*

9. *Twelve.*

10. *The blessing 'Sei benedica.'*

POST-SERIES LIVES

As E. Jack Neuman told *The TV Collector* magazine in their two-part 1994 interview/article, "The test of a series is that we're all still great friends, and that rarely happens in a series."[1]

Barry Newman has gone on to appear in about four dozen more films and television shows. One of those projects was a television mini-series entitled *Fatal Vision*, broadcast in 1984, in which he played a defense attorney very much like Petrocelli, vying with the prosecuting attorney played by Andy Griffith. Just as *The Lawyer* had given birth to *Petrocelli*, it was Griffith's role in *Fatal Vision* that led to his future *Matlock* series. NBC Entertainment president Brandon Tartikoff himself had seen the mini-series and dreamed of such a show for Andy. As a side note, we also see Albert Salmi as the judge in *Fatal Vision*. In 1989 Barry was a regular in the television series *Nightingales*. It's been his dream for years to produce movies about General Jack Pershing and Leonard Bernstein.

It was not long after the *Petrocelli* series wrapped that Susan Howard and Albert Salmi began a new project — the movie *Moonshine County Express*, released in 1977. Their roles in this film were quite different from those of their *Petrocelli* years: Susan was a moonshiner's daughter who, with her sisters, had inherited his business; and Albert was the sheriff. "Shine" must have been the working title because Albert had referred to it by that name when making a guest appearance on the husband-wife TV game show *Tattletales* during some downtime when he wasn't needed on the movie set.

Petrocelli producer/writer/director Leonard Katzman had wanted to cast Susan Howard as a regular in the very popular television series *Dallas*, of which he was also producer/writer/director. In 1979, he was

---

1. These two *The TV Collector* issues, No. 70 and 71, are still available at *www.angelfire.com/ma/tvcollector/home.html.*

able to do just that. Susan played the part of Donna Culver Krebbs in 198 episodes. A creative lady, Susan also contributed to the show by writing the episodes "Sitting Ducks" in 1986 and "The Ten Percent Solution" in 1987.

Above: This is what's left of the Indian Village Trading Post. What a terrible loss! *Below:* The Pima County Courthouse as it looks today.

CONCLUSION

Upon looking back on the television series that resulted from his movie, Sidney Furie said, "they reflected the flavor perfectly. . . . I think they featured Barry so well in every show. He was different than your average series lead. I was proud of what they did with my character."

Not only did Tucson's personality affect the show, but it seems that the show had an influence on its surroundings, too. Matt Welch said, "There was also an Italian restaurant called San Remo [San Remo Italian Dining, at 2210 N. Indian Ruins Road, Tucson] at the time, just down from where I live. Often wondered if there was any connection." There could very well have been a connection as Tony Petrocelli had been very proud of his Italian roots.

Now, four decades later, the Petrocelli sign in the window of the Indian Village Trading Post building is gone. The Trading Post had been managed for over sixty years by the Atkinson family, but the recession had caused a downturn in profits. The landlord would not lower the rent, so the Trading Post had to move out. The building is empty now. (Wouldn't lower rent have been preferable to no rent at all?)

The courthouse is still standing and is in the process of getting a facelift.

Much has changed, but *Petrocelli* is still fondly remembered by its fans. Thank goodness for TV Land and MeTV. They provided us with our *Petrocelli* fixes until the commercially-released DVD set was presented to the public in 2016. The feisty Anthony J. Petrocelli and beautiful, spunky Maggie are surely gaining new fans now from a new generation as they pass through the living room, see something interesting on TV, and ask, "What are you watching, Grandpa?"

SOURCES

Interviews with: Barry Newman, Susan Howard, and Steve Eastin
Correspondence from: James Sheldon, Steve Eastin, Sidney J. Furie, Lizanne Salmi Hanson, Jennifer Salmi LaRue, Matt Welch and Peter Mark Richman

BOOKS, NEWPAPERS, AND MAGAZINES:

Abilene Reporter-News
ALLSTAR project, Cesar Levy and Claudius Carnegie
Andy and Don: The Making of a Friendship and a Classic American TV Show (book by Daniel de Visé)
Asbury Park Press
Baton Rouge Advocate
Boston After Dark
Boston Herald American
Box Office
Bucks County Currier Times (Levittown, PA)
Charleston NC Evening Post
Courier-Journal (Louisville, KY)
Daily Independent Journal (San Rafael, CA)
Democrat (Little Rock, AR)
Duluth Sunday News-Tribune (Duluth, Minnesota)
Entertainment World
Film TV Daily
Florida Today (Cocoa, FL)
Hello, Darlin' (book by Larry Hagman)
High Point Enterprise (High Point, NC)
Hollywood Reporter
Hutchison (KS) *News*
Independent Press-Telegram (Long Beach, CA)
Indianapolis Star
Internet Movie Database
inter/VIEW
Irving Daily News (Irving, TX)
Journal Gazette (Mattoon, IL)
Journal News (White Plains, NY)
Kansas City Times
La Crosse Tribune (La Crosse, WI)

Los Angeles Times
Lexington Herald (Lexington, KY)
Lincoln Evening Journal (Lincoln, NE)
Morning News (Florence, SC)
Omaha World-Herald
Phildelphia Inquirer (Philadelphia, PA)
Pittsburgh Press
Post Star (Glen Falls, NY)
Poughkeepsie Journal (Poughkeepsie, NY)
Rennington VT Banner
Salinas Ranger Journal
San Diego Union (San Diego, CA)
Scottsdale (AZ) Daily Progress
Sunday Herald Advertiser (Boston, MA)
Telegraph (Alton, IL)
The Sunday Record
The Times Recorder
Tucson Daily Citizen
TV Collector magazine
Variety
Washington (DC) *Star-News*

BACKGROUND INFORMATION:

Max Allan Collins
Dan Gibson, Tucson Chamber of Commerce
Internet Movie Database
Bill Lawrence
Matt Welch

INDEX

Ackerman, Bettye 98
Aletter, Frank 100
Alexander, Dick 50
Alexander, Jane 24
Allen, Lee 91
Allman, Sheldon 113
Anderson, John 39, 48
Anderson Jr., Michael 70
Antonio, Jim 92
Archer, Anne 88, 89
Ardito, Gino 98
Ashley, Fred 50, 52, 64, 65, 91, 95
Atkinson Family 129
Bailey, F. Lee 18, 19
Barry, Don "Red" 83
Beatty, Ned 83, 84
Beir, Fred 67, 95
Bell, Michael 7, 70, 83, 84-85, 91, 94, 113
Benson, Lucille 57, 58, 68, 95, 109, 110
Bercovici, Leonard 41
Bernstein, Leonard 125
Bissell, Whit 111
Blair, Patricia 65, 67
Blood, Stephen T. 50, 59, 99
Blue Knight 79
Bond, Rudy 45
Bordon, Lynn 109
Brady, Barbara 42, 43
Brady, William 42, 43
Bramley, William 54, 68
Brennen, Claire 108
Brinegar, Paul 71
Brooke, Walter 48
Brothers Karamazov, The 22
Brown, Franklin 108
Bryant, Joshua 106

Buchman, Harold 33, 39
Bum Steer, The 28, 29, 60
Burke, Paul 106, 107
Burnett, Mary-Nancy 113
Burns, Michael 52
Butkus, Dick 94
Calhoun, Rory 45
Calomee, Gloria 98
Campanella, Joseph 41
Cannon 79
Cardi, Ray 103
Carlin, Lynn 47
Carr, Paul 60
Carson, John David 55, 56
Casey, Lawrence 100
Casper, Gary Mike 83
Chorbanian, Aram 67, 87
Chrane, Calvin 23, 81
Clarke, Angela 55, 87
Cobb, Julie 60
Colbert, Robert 33
Coleman, Dabney 111
Colicos, John 92
Collier, Marian 7
Collins, Max Allan 7, 15
Comer, Anjanette 67
Conaway, Michele 59
Congress Hotel (aka Hotel Congress) 48, 49
Connolly, Christopher 61, 62, 101, 102
Corbett, Glenn 47, 87
Coriell, Eugene F. 48
Costello, Ward 108
Cox, John H. 85, 88
Crawford, John 71, 83
Crawford, Oliver 43
Crothers, Scatman 113, 114

Crowley, Kathleen 33
Cunningham, Shirley 39
Curtis, Ken 100
Cypher, Jon 36
Dallas 82, 125-126
Dano, Linda 111
Darby, Kim 65, 66
Darrow, Henry 36
Daugherty, Herschel 64
Daughton, James 104, 105
David, Thayer 103
Davison, Davey 99
Dawson, John 73
DeBenning, Burr 111
DeCamp, Rosemary 90
Dehner, John 64
Dennis, Robert C. 52, 65
Deuel, Geoffrey 48
Dexter, Brad 33
Dey, Susan 100
Dillinger, John 50
Doherty, James 48
Donahue, Elinor 70
Donner, Richard 50
Douglas, Mike 81
Doyle, David 43
Dubbins, Donald 67
Dusay, Marj 94
Earle, Gene 64, 68, 70
Eastin, Steve 7, 59, 60, 87, 98, 99, 106
Eilbacher, Bobby 67
Elcar, Dana 47
Elliott, Stephen 73
Elman, Richard 50, 67
Enriquez, Rene 101
Episodes:
   Season One:
   Ep 1 — "The Golden Cage" 41
   Ep 2 — "Music to Die By" 43
   Ep 3 — "By Reason of Madness" 16, 45
   Ep 4 — "Edge of Evil" 47
   Ep 5 — "A Life For a Life" 48
   Ep 6 — "Death in High Places" 50
   Ep 7 — "The Double Negative" 52
   Ep 8 — "Mirror, Mirror on the Wall" 16, 54
   Ep 9 — "An Act of Love" 55
   Ep 10 — "A Very Lonely Lady" 16, 57
   Ep 11 — "Counterploy" 59
   Ep 12 — "A Covenant With Evil" 16, 60

   Ep 13 — "The Sleep of Reason" 61
   Ep 14 — "A Fallen Idol" 63
   Ep 15 — "Once Upon a Victim" 64
   Ep 16 — "The Kidnapping" 65
   Ep 17 — "A Lonely Victim" 67
   Ep 18 — "The Outsiders" 68
   Ep 19 — "Vengeance in White" 70
   Ep 20 — "Four the Hard Way" 71
   Ep 21 — "Death in Small Doses" 73
   Ep 22 — "A Night of Terror" 76
   Season Two:
   Ep 1 — "Death Ride" 83
   Ep 2 — "Mark of Cain" 85
   Ep 3 — "Five Yards of Trouble" 87
   Ep 4 — "Shadow of Fear" 88
   Ep 5 — "Chain of Command" 90
   Ep 6 — "To See No Evil" 91
   Ep 7 — "Terror on Wheels" 92
   Ep 8 — "The Gamblers" 93
   Ep 9 — "Terror by the Book" 94
   Ep 10 — "Face of Evil" 16, 95
   Ep 11 — "Too Many Alibis" 98
   Ep 12 — "A Deadly Vow" 99
   Ep 13 — "The Falling Star" 100
   Ep 14 — "Survival" 101
   Ep 15 — "The Night Visitor" 103
   Ep 16 — "Blood Money" 104
   Ep 17 — "Any Number Can Die" 106
   Ep 18 — "Six Strings of Guilt" 108
   Ep 19 — "Deadly Journey" 109
   Ep 20 — "The Pay Off" 111
   Ep 21 — "Shadow of a Doubt" 112
   Ep 22 — "Jubilee Jones" 113
Evans, Gene 65
Ewing, Diana 83
Farrell, Sharon 48
Farringer, Lisa 52
Fatal Vision 125
Fear is the Key 20
Fisher, Art 101
Flory, Med 76
Ford, Harrison 47
Forestal, Sean 112
Forsyth, Rosemary 40, 41, 43, 99
Foster, Meg 22
Foster, Ron 87, 100
Francis, Anne 94, 95
Franklin, Pamela 61
Freiberger, Fred 98

INDEX

French, Victor 111, 112, 113
Fudge, Alan 64, 76
Furie, Sydney 7, 15, 19, 33, 39, 129
Gammon, James 104
George, Lynda Day 45
Get Christie Love 29, 79
Gibson, Marian 98
Gilford, Gwynne 106
Ging, Jack 57, 93
Gleason, Lowell 67
Goddard, Mark 67, 111
Goldberg, Mel 47
Goldsmith, Jonathan 65
Gordon, Mark 106
Gordon, William D. 48
Gossett Jr., Louis 57, 63
Gould, Harold 16, 20, 33, 50, 52, 53, 54, 112
Grayson, Kurt 54
Green, Bob 60
Griffith, Andy 125
Hagen, Erica 54, 91
Hagman, Larry 82
Hamill, Mark 68, 69, 93
Hammer, Ben 63
Hammond, Nicholas 104
Hamner, Earl 89
Hardy, Robert E. 47
Harens, Dean 60
Harley, Bill 60
Harrington, Tammy 108
Hart, Christina 55
Harter, Chuck 7
Hatunen, Dave 91
Hellstrom, Gunnar 65
Helmond, Katherine 112
High Chaparral 21
Hill, Riley 98
Hodge, Bob 24
Hollywood Squares, The 81
Hooks, Robert 98
Howard, Susan 7, 9, 10, 11, 12, 15, 22, 23, 26, 36, 40 *(+ in each episode cast list)*, 42, 46, 75, 80, 81, 102, 107, 115, 116, 121, 123, 125-126
Huddleston, David 43, 44, 52, 60, 67, 104, 106
Hudock, John 93, 108, 113
Huston, Gaye 59
Indian Village Trading Post 21, 128, 129
Jacome, Richard 87
Jacome's 30

Jarrett, Renne 64
Jarvis, Francesca 70, 90, 106
Jeffers, Arnold 51, 59, 60, 65, 87, 91, 95, 98, 99, 100
Jens, Salome 99
Jones, Caro 21
Jones, Henry 48
Kato McShane 79
Katzman, Leonard 24, 41, 45, 47, 48, 50, 52, 54, 55, 57, 59, 60, 61, 63, 64, 65, 67, 68, 70, 71, 76, 82, 82, 83, 85, 87, 88, 90, 91, 92, 93, 94, 95, 98, 99, 100, 101, 103, 104, 106, 108, 109, 111, 112, 113, 115, 125
Kavner, Julie 91, 92
Kelley, William 45, 61, 71, 76
Kelly, Eugene 93
Kemmerling, Warren J. 33, 88, 99
Kendrick, Henry 95
Kenyon, Sandy 43
Keys, Williams 87
Kirkland, Sally 98
Koslo, Paul 85
Kove, Martin 108
Landers, Alan 99
Larson, Darrell 104
Lasko, Edward J. 59
Launer, S. John 94
Lawyer, The 15, 19, 20, 52, 123
LeDesma, Hector 45
Lefcourt, Peter 92
LeGault, Lance 76
Lenz, Kay 95, 96, 97
LeRoy, Gloria 71, 101
Lessing, Norman 104
Libby, Brian 112
Lippe, Jonathan 64, 65, 88, 101
London, Jerry 112
Lookinland, Todd 65
Lucas Tanner 29, 79
Luna, Barbara 87
Lupton, John 90, 93
Lynch, Paul 109
Lyons, Robert F. 95
MacRae, Elizabeth 73
Maggio, Donell-Di 109
Malet, Arthur 60
Mandan, Robert 73, 74
Manhunter 29, 79
Manners, Sam 46
Marie, Rose 41

Marley, John 55
Martel, Arlene 57
Martin, Dewey 94
Martin, Strother 71
Martinez, A 93
Masters, Ben 59
Matheson, Tim 112, 113
Matlock 125
Mayberry, Russ 100
McCarthy, Lin 90
McEachin, James 45
McEveety, Bernard 76
McEveety, Vincent 57
McNaughton Rule 45
McRaney, Gerald 83, 92
Meeker, Ralph 36
Mell, Joseph 76
Michaelian, Katharyn 83, 90
Michaelian, Michael 90
Miles, Joanna 108
Milford, John 57
Milkis, Edward K. 24, 36, 39, 43
Millan, Robyn 60
Miller, Thomas L. 24, 36, 39, 43, 68, 91, 95
Mitchell, Cameron 50
Montgomery, Belinda 50
Montgomery, Lee H. 90
Moonshine County Express 125
Moore, Irving J. 47, 54, 61, 67, 68, 83, 88, 91, 94, 95, 99, 104
Moore, Joanna 111
Morheim, Lou 43, 73
Mosley, Moe 101, 103, 108
Most, Donny 111
Muldaur, Diana 20, 33, 35
Myrow, Jeff 106
Nelson, Rick 43, 44
Nettleton, Lois 76, 77
Neuman, E. Jack 7, 19, 22, 23, 36, 39, 108, 109, 125
Neuman, Mrs. E. Jack (See Marian Collier)
Nevins, Claudette 55
Newman, Barry 7, 9, 10, 11, 12, 16, 18, 19, 20, 22, 24, 25, 28-29, 32, 34, 35, 40 *(+ in each episode cast list)*, 42, 44, 46, 53, 56, 62, 66, 73, 75, 78, 79, 80, 81, 85, 86, 89, 100, 102, 108, 115, 116, 117, 118, 119, 121, 123, 125
Night Games 7, 20, 25, 26
Odets, Clifford 24
O'Hanlon, Jr., George 73

O'Hara, Maureen 20
Oliver, Susan 47
Orlandi, Felice 48
O'Toole, Annette 92
Paull, Morgan 47
Pershing, General Jack 125
Petrie, George 63, 100
Petrocelli, Mama 12, 44, 54, 102, 121, 122
Pevney, Joseph 41, 71, 87, 111
Phillips, Barney 50
Pima County Courthouse 25-26, 27, 119, 128, 129
Pine, Phillip 103
Pipkin, Leo 50
Poliakoff, Shirley 95
Powers, Stephanie 36, 38, 54
Prince, William 112
Pyle, Denver 104, 105
Rainey, Ford 83
Ramirez, Monika 93
Ramsey, Logan 61
Raymond, Lina 71
Reese, Della 64
Rendina, Victor 88
Reisner, Allen 48
Reynolds, Al 73
Rhoades, Barbara 113
Rhue, Madlyn 67
Richards, Beah 113
Richman, Peter Mark 76, 77
Riskin, Ralph 39
Rist, Robbie 87, 88
Ritter, John 90
Robbins, Bernie 43
Roberts, Stanley 64
Roland, Paul 92, 99
Rorke, Hayden 59
Rosenthal, Sandy 95, 99
Ross, Marian 68, 109
Rubin, Andrew 104
Rubin, Mann 111
Russell, Bing 94
Ruymen, Ayn 92
Salmi Hansen, Lizanne 7, 27, 83-84
Salmi LaRue, Jennifer 7, 83
Salmi, Albert 7, 9, 10, 12, 15, 22, 26-28, 36, 40 *(+ in each episode cast list)*, 46, 66, 73, 75, 80, 83, 121, 125
Salzberg Connection, The 20
Sandor, Steve 91

INDEX

Saxon, John 85, 86
Scott, Brenda 70
Scott, Simon 55, 67
Scott, Timothy 104
Shatner, William 47
Sheerer, Robert 103
Sheldon, James 7, 28, 45, 46, 59, 60
Shepard, Dalice 7
Sheppard, Dr. Sam case 19, 34
Silver-Kramer, Deena 94
Slate, Jeremy 43
Smith, Charles Martin 60
Stanley, Paul 43, 55
Starr, Don 43, 44, 59, 92, 104, 111
Starsky & Hutch 79
Stevens, Warren 90
Stewart, Hayes 68
Stone, Norman 95
Strasberg, Susan 63
Stratton, Albert 61
Stromsoe, Fred 41
Stroud, Don 63, 64
Stull, Robert 57, 70
Sullivan, Susan 98
Swit, Loretta 45
Swofford, Ken 16, 33, 70, 85, 103
Tartikoff, Brandon 125
Tattletales 125
Taylor, Don 36, 73
Thatcher, Torin 73
Tippit, Wayne 108
Tobey, Kenneth 90
Townshende, Robb 57

Tyburn, Gene 52
Ullman, Daniel B. 41, 47
Van Ark, Joan 103
Vanishing Point 20, 100
Vernon, John 45
Vint, Alan 109
Vogel, Mitch 68
Wallerstein, Herb 52, 63, 90, 92, 93, 98
Ward, Richard 63
Wayland, Len 99
Weaver, Fritz 52, 53
Wednesday Movie of the Week 79
Weis, Don 108
Welch, Matt 29, 129
Welsh, Thomas 30, 39
Wesson, Dick 113
Whitman, Kipp 92
Wiers, James J. 87
Wiggins, Russell 57
Wilcox, Mary 33
Williams, Cindy 101
Williams, Jack 43
Williams, Vera 43
Willingham, Nobel 100
Wilson, Ned 94
Windom, William 41, 88, 89
Woodward, Morgan 40, 41, 76
Woolsey, Ralph 32
Wynant, H. M. 87
Yokley, Richard 7
York, Francine 61, 100
Young, Charles 68, 93
Zenor, Suzanne 100, 104

Bear Manor Media

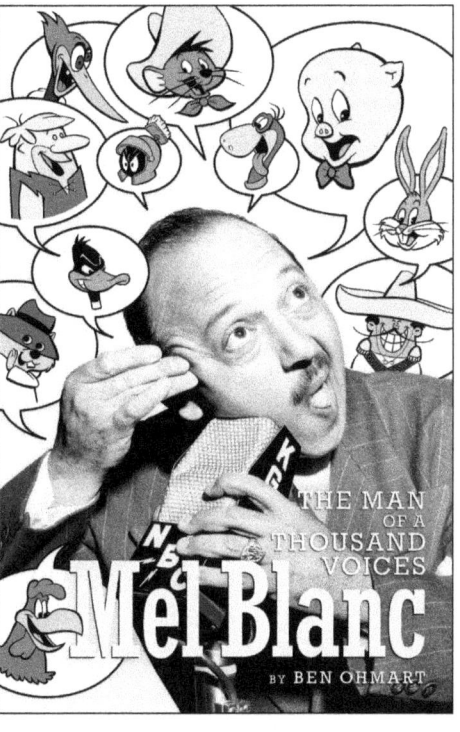
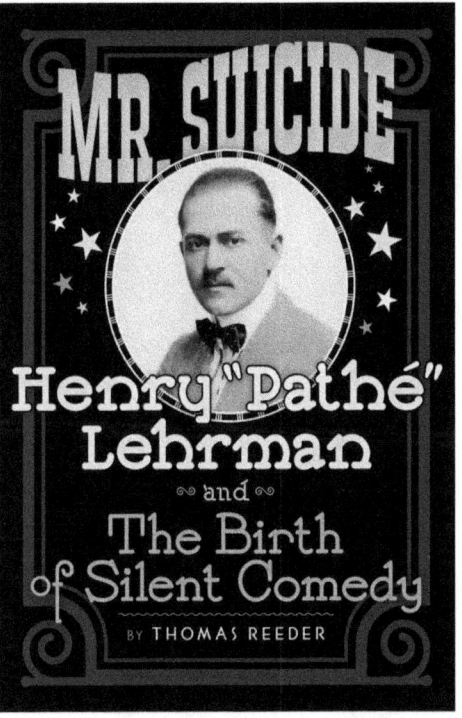

Classic Cinema.
Timeless TV.
Retro Radio.
WWW.BEARMANORMEDIA.COM

www.ingramcontent.com/pod-product-compliance
Lightning Source LLC
Chambersburg PA
CBHW071125090426
42736CB00012B/2014